The Wildman of Kentucky

The Mystery of Panther Rock

By Philip Spencer

The Wildman of Kentucky: The Mystery of Panther Rock
Copyright© 2008 by Reality Press and Philip Spencer. All rights reserved.

Reality Press
An imprint of Reality Entertainment, Inc.

For information contact:

REALITY ENTERTAINMENT
P.O. Box 91
Foresthill, CA 95631

Ph: 530-367-5389
Fx: 530-367-3024

www.reality-entertainment.com

ISBN: 978-1-934588-38-3

Printed in the United States of America.

CONTENTS

FOREWORD BY O.H. KRILL

There is probably no other unknown creature that arouses more curiosity than the Bigfoot or Sasquatch. Yes, there is the Loch Ness Monster, the Chupacabra and other great beasts of lore, but the Bigfoot remains the most compelling as it pulls us toward ourselves, shadowing the unknown X factor of our very origins. The case files contain thousands of reported sightings, yet no actual specimen has ever been found. Hundreds of photographs exist, but the creature has not been identified. Still, the clues accumulate year after year. In the words of one Bigfoot investigator, "It is an extremely complex phenomenon with no starting point and few geographical limits." If this creature does exist then it most certainly must be a relative of man.

Descriptions of the ape-like creature do not vary dramatically with credible sightings. The creature is anywhere from six to ten feet tall, 300 to 1,000 pounds and walks upright on two legs. Hair covers almost all of its body and ranges in color from black to silvery white, with the predominant color being brown or reddish brown. The creature is often reported to have a flat face and nose, a receding, sloped forehead with a prominent brow ridge and a cone-shaped head which sits on broad shoulders with no apparent neck. Its proportions are roughly those of a human, except for its long, dangling arms. Bigfoot draws its name from the enormous footprints it leaves behind, many as long as two feet by eight inches wide. The length of stride varies, but the distance is usually close to four feet between prints. There have been group sightings, one or more adults and one or sometimes multiple juveniles in tow. The creatures are thought to be largely nocturnal.

Species? Unknown at this time.

Thousands of Indian locations are named after the "Boss of the Mountain" or the "Wild Man" as the Bigfoot was originally called by the

Amerindians. Indian cultures generally regard the Wild Man with the greatest respect. He is viewed as a special kind of being, perhaps because of his seemingly close relationship to humans. Many Indian elders regard him as standing on the "border" between animal and human consciousness, giving him a supernatural, special kind of power. Many Indian cultures view Wild Man encounters as a deeply spiritual experience. But as special as he may be, there is no tribe that suggests that he is anything other than a physical being, living in the same physical dimensions as humans and other animals. He eats, sleeps, gathers and communicates with family members.

Wild Man or Sasquatch attributes from numerous reports.

The smell of a Sasquatch far exceeds that of a bear or other mammals, many cases report an intolerable stench when a Bigfoot is in the area.

They vocalize in terrifyingly, high pitched scream like mannerisms, many recordings have surfaced in recent years.

They knock trees, possibly to communicate with each other over long distances.

They throw rocks and boulders. There are many reported cases where a Bigfoot threw rocks at campers, even boulders from hilltops if disturbed.

They live in family units. Many cases report the sighting of not one but two or more individuals at a time, often with young in tow.

They wash their food. In 1924, Albert Ostman was abducted by a Bigfoot, and then held captive by a family unit. He noted, among other things, the female Bigfoot washing and stacking leaves and vegetation. This behavior has been reported multiple times in the last 100 years.

They may have developed a language. Many reports tell of a whinnying or gurgling whistle sound associated with their possible speech patterns.

Hundreds of Bigfoot or Sasquatch footprints have been found and preserved in castings all over the world, but in recent years, the enigma of the Bigfoot has taken a very profound leap. The Bigfoot has dermal ridges.

Definition:
A friction ridge is a raised portion of the epidermis on the palm and fingers of the hand, or the soul and toes of the foot. They consist of one or more connected ridge units of friction ridge skin. These ridges are also known as "dermal ridges." The three basic patterns of fingerprint ridges are the arch, loop, and whorl.

Many Bigfoot castings clearly show dermal ridges not unlike those found in humans. If the Bigfoot phenomenon is a prank or a hoax, it is one of the greatest hoaxes of all time. The best prints on record were found in extremely remote places. To leave these prints and artificially create dermal ridges would be extremely difficult to say the least. When gorillas were first seen by white men early in the last century, the reaction to the discovery was one of shock and astonishment. Native stories of such creatures were well-known but were viewed as mere folklore and mythology by the scientific community. Prior to this paleontological milestone, man had the idea that he had more or less discovered everything there was to discover about ourselves.

Let us not take lightly that Gigantopithecus, was a very real creature. Gigantopithecus is an extinct genus of ape that existed from roughly one million years to as recently as three hundred thousand years ago in what is now China, India, and Vietnam which places Gigantopithecus in the same time frame and geographical location as several hominoid species. The fossil record suggests that the Gigantopithecus blacki species were the largest apes that ever lived. Standing up to 10 ft. and weighing up to 1,200 pounds makes the species two to three times heavier than modern gorillas and nearly five times heavier than the orangutan, its closest living relative. Evidence of a separate species, Gigantopithecus giganteus, has been found in northern India and China. Fossils of teeth and mandibles from Gigantopithecus blacki have been found in cave sites in Southeast Asia. Recent research using high-precision dating methods has shown that after existing for about a million years, Gigantopithecus blacki died out 100,000 years ago. This means that it coexisted with modern humans (Homo Sapiens) for thousands of years, and with the most immediate ancestors of Homo Sapiens before that. Many cryptozoologists believe Gigantopithecines are the legendary primates known in various geographic locations as Bigfoot, Yowie, Yeren, or Yeti but these claims are not considered credible by the scientific community.

Although the Wildman has been most frequently seen in the Pacific Northwest, sightings are by no means limited to that area, they are in fact worldwide and remarkably consistent from case to case with regard to many attributes and mannerisms reported by the eyewitnesses involved. Bigfoot sightings occur in many places not often attributed to being "hot spots" but more and more eyewitnesses are coming forward. One such witness is a gentleman by the name of Lynn Hutton, an upstanding citizen of the great state of Kentucky, the blue grass state and home of the Kentucky Derby. Mr. Hutton, Bruce Young and others in Kentucky have had incredible encounters with the creature known as Bigfoot that are detailed in this book as well as the film of the same name.

Oddly enough, giant skeletons have been found in Kentucky. In Mammoth Cave, the skeleton of an 8 foot tall giant was found along with a smaller adolescent in 1811. In 1876, The New York Times ran an article that referred to remains of three 8 foot giants found in the state. In 1965, landowner Kenneth White, was building cattle stalls when under a ledge he found a perfectly preserved skeleton which measured 8 feet, 9 inches in length when reassembled. He states, "The arms were extremely long and the hands were large. The skull was 30 inches in circumference. The eye and nose sockets were slits rather than cavities, and the area where the jawbone hinges to the skull was solid bone."

Over the past 200 years or more, Bigfoot sightings as well as other anomalous phenomena have been reported at a place called Panther Rock in Anderson County, Kentucky. The area you are about to journey to with the author, has been known to Indians, pioneers and early settlers as "The Dark and Bloody Ground" well before we came to know it as The Frazier Land. Read on my friends and you shall learn the reasons why so many Kentuckians have nothing but respect for this place and why so many god fearing people believe there is such a thing as Bigfoot.

From a letter found in the Kentucky Library dated 1840:

"It was on a cold night in the blue hills of Kentucky, we felt a presence that was undeniable in this place ... where moon shiners and trappers roamed after the Indians were long gone, we heard the scream of the Wild Man... Indeed we knew we were trespassers in his world now. There are no human conveniences here, no sheriff to call, just the wilderness in its perfect and unyielding state. The Amerindians say he was here long, long before them and long before any white man came to this valley. We heard that scream, the unearthly, deafening, scream that unequivocally let us know that this was not our domain and that all the 'progress' man had made meant absolutely nothing in this place."

PREFACE

Just after daylight I picked up my Stevens Crack Shot rifle and headed back into our land on our farm in Alton Kentucky, located in Anderson County. A young boy walking along the open fields and headed for the woods to try and bring home some food. As I walked I came to a hilltop and walked into the open field. The field had given its last bit of food for the year and had been plowed under and then smoothed with a drag. As I walked I looked at the land around me, I looked at the dew on the ground and I thought how fall was close and it was now taking the life from all the plants and trees and how the cycle was never ending. I walked into the field and as I came to the middle of this field I noticed something in the dirt. At first I thought it was just a place where perhaps a groundhog had disturbed the dirt or maybe even a rabbit had dug.

But as I came up close to the disturbance in the ground I soon realized I was not seeing either, I was looking at a footprint. Even as a young boy in this area of Kentucky you learn about the outdoors early in life, you learn how to track and hunt and fish and you learn about nature. What my eyes were locked on was something I had never seen before and something I knew instantly was out of place. I stood and looked the track over carefully. It was a right foot and it was large, it was approximately 12 to 14 inches in length, and it had only three toes. The ground was nearly perfect to take the track of something with weight and this track was distinct and easy to see. So there I stood in the middle of this field staring at this strange three toed footprint and thinking to myself what could have made this track?

This field was not a huge piece of land and in size I would say it covered maybe 8 acres. It was not a problem to see every inch of this field and I looked over all the area surrounding the footprint to see if other tracks could be seen, there were none. Years later I found the website of Pennsylvania investigator and author Stan Gordon, and he had a picture of a cast of a three toed track or maybe it was a picture of the track itself. As time went on I heard others speak of the three toed tracks in association with Bigfoot and in numerous instances, they told of only finding one impression. This was the only time I ever saw a track like this but it was an event that stayed with me always and pointed me and guided me to my search for what many call the abnormal side of existence.

Casual conversations sometimes lead to amazing stories, which is the case of "The Frazier Land." It began with a conversation between two old friends when one mentioned he possessed a photo of a very strange animal footprint. As someone who for over 40 years has researched, read and been somewhat obsessed with the paranormal and all of its unusual glory, my interest was immediately peaked. My friend described a photo he took of a strange animal track including details of how it was taken and how it was found. I asked if he could show me a copy of the image and he said he would have to find it. Finding the image turned into a quest of its own but in time it was found. My friend emailed me the image and as soon as my eyes looked upon it I knew this was something unusual. And so with my viewing of this picture, with its single track, began this story of The Frazier Land and of Panther Rock, and The Wildman Of Kentucky.

The Frazier Land is located in Anderson County Kentucky, with the town of Lawrenceburg as the county seat. Lawrenceburg is a beautiful, small country town with great food and friendly people, surrounded by the beauty of nature. Rivers, streams, creeks, lakes, gorgeous valleys, rolling hillsides and everything one could want in a place to live and enjoy life and enjoy nature. The exact amount of land that exists in this area known as The Frazier Land is unknown, but it consists of thousands of acres. The name "The Frazier Land" is known mostly by the old ones, and the specific reasoning for this area being called by this name is unknown to me or anyone I have talked to about it. But what is known is that this area of land holds many mysteries and many stories. From large black cats to Bigfoot, from strange rock formations to mysterious lights, apparitions to evil, The Frazier Land holds it all. This land lies on the plateaus of the Kentucky River and is a mixture of farm land and wilderness. Many streams run down from the hills and feed the river. To say the area is beautiful would be a huge understatement. The water coming down from the hills cuts numerous channels in the hillsides which are often covered with moss. Streams are abundant, and wildlife is plentiful. The terrain is rocky and tough to traverse, and the woodlands are thick with brush and trees of many types. Due to the limestone content of the earth in this area, caves are abundant.

Before we start discussing the stories associated with this area, let us get to know the central point of all these strange events. That area is called Panther Rock and it features a limestone cave located on private property and secluded from view by the surrounding woods.

The tales of Panther Rock are many, such as where the name Panther Rock came from. As the story goes many years ago a Native American chief was killed at the cave. Late one night a family who lived in a small cabin nearby heard screams and the sounds of a large cat attacking someone or something. The next morning the man walked to Panther Rock and found the chief's dead body which was ripped to shreds.

This is how the old ones say Panther Rock received its name. So many unusual and strange stories surround Panther Rock that it is hard not to think that the cave is the center of all this activity. If someone were to lay out a map and place Panther Rock as the center point then go outward and mark areas where these strange events take place, it would be very easy to consider Panther Rock the focal point of all these events. My personal opinion is that Panther Rock is the central point of these events and it is somehow tied to all the events in this area. How or why it is, well, that is a question that I cannot answer, but I will present the stories of The Frazier Land and Panther Rock and let you think about the whys, whats, ifs and maybes of this intriguing story.

I have heard the tales of the area for years and I have also had two personal experiences at Panther Rock. It was these personal experiences, combined with all the other strange information that I had gathered about this area of Kentucky, that made me decide to tell this story and share it with all those who find these type of events captivating. The tales of Bigfoot and large black cats as well as other strange occurrences are abundant in our society. Stories of a large, hairy creature of immense size wandering the land have been told for many years. Are they folk tales to scare the young ones, myths, or are they factual and true? Until we have something that proves beyond any doubt that these events and creatures are real, we will have endless debates and endless arguments over the validity of these stories. From the Northeast to the Southeast and out to the Midwest and beyond, the stories of large black cats have prevailed for years. And from the same areas the stories of a large, hairy, manlike, creature roaming the land have been told for hundreds of years along with the tales of ghosts and other paranormal events.

So what do we think about all these tales? A line in a song by Radney Foster states, "Real life can always use a good stretch." We tend to be storytellers and we also tend to "stretch" the stories to make them better. This is not a malicious act, it is simply the way people are. Yes sometimes greed and stupidity take over and individuals make up stories in an attempt to profit, but in most cases it is just the tales around the campfire that are embellished over time. And so in lies a real problem. When someone sees something that is not supposed to exist or has an encounter that is so out of this world they do not know how to explain it, it is soon demoted to a tall tale and in many cases the person is ridiculed and humiliated. So a real life event of strangeness is delegated almost immediately to nothing more than someone making up a story to draw attention to themselves or to just make up a story. The sad result of this is that an endless amount of information is lost. People will see strange creatures and have strange and bizarre events occur and they will never tell anyone. The story will remain theirs and maybe get shared with a trusted friend but never told publicly. Because of this, valuable information remains hidden that could hold the key to the truth concerning these elusive animals which are much sought after.

Although you will find many who damn the internet, it has been a tremendous tool for information to be presented to the masses and once done so; investigators can then tear into the story and try to determine if the story is fact or fiction. Some who live in The Frazier Land have no idea of all that has happened over the years, of the strangeness happening all around them. Yet these individuals could have had something happen and just kept it to themselves without realizing they were part of the mysteries of Panther Rock and The Frazier Land. Perhaps you will find the clues that lead to the answer. Or perhaps you will do like most, sit and wonder what in the world is going on in this area and has been going on for many years. How could all this occur and still no one has a clue as to what is causing it or why it is occurring? But one thing is certain to those who know The Frazier Land - when the night falls and darkness covers the land, avoid being alone. Keep your doors locked and just stay inside when the sounds come, stay inside when the unexplained comes in the dark, just let it be. And for certain, if the darkness calls you, do not answer; don't be lured into The Frazier Land by yourself.

I want to thank all those who have taken the time and effort to seek the truth, without letting others stand in their way, and understanding that we as a people are not the absolute last word in what is reality and what is not. Numerous new species are found every year while the human species is so self-destructive there is a good chance we will destroy ourselves over time. Or perhaps one day a dedicated researcher will find the answer to all these "paranormal" events, and find the reason for all the sightings of creatures which are not supposed to exist, or why the shadows move in the night. And within these answers will be the key to saving us from ourselves. Let us all hope that one day strange will be normal.

Philip Spencer

A HISTORICAL GLANCE

Many discussions have occurred trying to determine where Kentucky got its name and what the word Kentucky means. Many times it has been written that it means "the dark and bloody ground," however if you check Wikipedia here is the information they provide:

"The origin of Kentucky's name (variously spelled Cane-tuck-ee, Cantucky, Kain-tuck-ee, and Kentuckee before its modern spelling was accepted) [5] has never been definitively identified, though some theories have been debunked. For example, Kentucky's name does not come from the combination of "cane" and "turkey"; and though it is the most popular belief, it is unlikely to mean "dark and bloody ground" because it isn't found in any known Indian language.[6] The most likely etymology is that it comes from an Iroquoian word for "meadow" or "prairie" [7][8] (c.f. Mohawk kenhtà:ke, Seneca këhta'keh). [9] Other possibilities also exist: the suggestion of early Kentucky pioneer George Rogers Clark that the name means "the river of blood", [5] a Wyandot name meaning "land of tomorrow", a Shawnee term possibly referring to the head of a river, [10] or an Algonquian word for a river bottom. [6]"

The definition of the word Kentucky may be debated for many years, but one thing that will not be debated is just how prolific the stories are of strange creatures and other unusual events taking place in the bluegrass state. Kentucky is a land of enormous beauty and mystery. From the west to the east and north to the south, as one looks back into the past of this majestic state so many mysteries and amazing stories are available it is hard to know where to start. From the burial ground of people over seven feet tall to the strange snake mounds, to the numerous stories of large solid black cats who have been seen by many. Tales are told in the valleys, mountains, along the streams and by the campfires at night. Reports of large, hairy, manlike creatures go back many years and tell of a group of these creatures who were heard yelling Yeahoh over and over. There is even a tale of the legendary Daniel Boone killing a large, hairy, creature in the woods which he called a "Yahoo," and which was said to be over ten feet tall. This story is very likely related to the creatures in Jonathan Swift's book *Gulliver's Travels*. Swift wrote of these large, hairy, manlike creatures and called them Yahoos. It is also stated that *Gulliver's Travels* was a favorite book of Daniel Boone.

There are numerous reported Bigfoot sightings in Kentucky. Moreover, the number of sightings of large, hairy, manlike creatures worldwide is not only enormous, but many go back hundreds and even thousands of years. Following is a sample report from 1899:

Major Laurence Austine Waddel of the Indian Army Medical Corps found large footprints in the snow of the Himalayas at 17,000 feet. He wrote: "These were alleged to be the trail of the hairy wild men who are believed to live amongst the eternal snows, along with the mythical white lions, whose roar is reputed to be heard during storms. The belief in these creatures is universal among Tibetans."

- From *Among the Himalayas* (1899) by Major Waddel.

The name Wildman and its association with the creature known now as Bigfoot goes back to ancient times. Numerous accounts from around the world refer to a large, hairy, manlike creature and the name used in referring to this creature is Wildman. Reports from AD 618-970 of a creature called yeh-ren, a bipedal creature with 14 to 16 inch feet. There are numerous other instances where ogres or the "Wildmen of the woods" are mentioned in ancient Chinese literature.

In Tibet - Osodrashin
In China - Peey
In Mongolia - Zerleg-khoon
In central Asia - Almas
In the United States - Bigfoot
In most of Canada - Sasquatch
In Canada (Quebec) - Windigo

In Japan - Hibagon
In South America - Mapinguary
In India, Tibet & Nepal - Yeti

And the list goes on.

Sasquatch is a common name used in the United States and other countries such as Canada for this illusive, upright, bipedal, hairy hominoid creature that holds the fascination of so many people. The word Sasquatch is derived from the Salish Indian word "Sesquac" which means "Wildman."

Worldwide the phenomenon of a huge, manlike, hairy creature is part of not only our history, but our various cultures. With tens of thousands of sightings going back into ancient times, at some point we must stop and ask ourselves exactly what is going on with this phenomenon. Are all these sighting and reports just visualizations of over active psychological manifestations of the human mind? Or is this creature actually out there? The hard evidence on hand as of this writing is scarce and inconclusive. But as time goes on more scientific ways of analyzing the evidence will come into play, and with these advanced techniques perhaps one day the answer will be found. But we must not discount or discard the simple fact that one day soon this creature may just walk out of the woods and be seen by a large number of people. Or perhaps we are not meant to ever know what this creature is, perhaps we are being watched, maybe we are being studied?

Reports of large black cats are plentiful in the history of Kentucky, and to this day are still reported. These cats are reported to be melanistic and simply written off as a freak of nature with its genes confused. And in many cases the reports are simply denied as being invalid and thus ignored and never looked into. Since 1939 approximately 13 melanistic bobcats have been captured or killed in Florida. These cats are not as big as a cougar/panther but show that large black cats most certainly exist.

However this does not explain the strangeness of the sighting of large black cats in many areas. In many cases the reports mention oddities in regard to the size or to events associated with the sighting. One such event is when a mysterious black cat is sighted a Bigfoot sighting is often reported within the same time frame or soon after. A linkage between the two has never been made but one has to wonder if there is some out of world connection between these two creatures. Even UFO reports have had the elusive Bigfoot associated with their sightings.

In 1931 a book was published with the title *Panther Rock*. The author of the book was Arin Bond Burr. Very few copies of this book are known to exist. To read the book one must go to the Anderson Public Library as it cannot be taken out due to its rareness and in order to preserve it. The book is a wonderful piece of literature and a real glance into history and what life was like for the first people who lived in the area of Panther Rock. Within the book is the tale previously mentioned of the Native American chief who was killed by a panther above the cave which resulted in the cave being named Panther Rock. Another story tells of the night when the residents heard a loud gurgling sound as if a huge amount of water was running out of something and the next morning they came outside to find the small lake was gone, vanished into the earth in the middle of the night. But perhaps the most interesting statements in the book are vague in nature. It is mentioned how the elderly would sit and tell the children the stories of Panther Rock and how the stories would frighten them. The time frame for these stories seems to be from the mid 1700's until the 1800's, which means Panther Rock has been the source of strange tales for many years.

The cave, Panther Rock, has a unique quality to it. You can feel something when you are near it. Historically a waterfall above the mouth of the cave fell over 200 feet into the Kentucky River. Now the cave just suddenly appears in the middle of a beautiful landscape hidden from view. This cave holds many secrets and like a good gambler, it keeps those secrets close to its vest. Tales are told of dogs that went into the cave and came out hundreds of miles away. A circle marks the top of the cave and this circle has been there for as long as anyone can remember. These same type circles can be found on farms that adjoin the Panther Rock area. Inside these circles nothing will grow the same as it grows in the surrounding areas. Even in the densest woods, only grass will grow within the circles and yet it doesn't grow like the other grass in the area. Within just a few miles of the cave, animals have been attacked and never seen again, and animal tracks have been found in the mud but no one can say for certain exactly what made them. Sounds have been recorded that make you feel cold as you listen to them. And many more events have occurred within The Frazier Land and surrounding the cave known as Panther Rock. Perhaps Kentucky was not known as "the dark and bloody ground." However in Bond's book, *Panther Rock*, the term "the dark and bloody ground" was mentioned. So perhaps we have found the dark and bloody ground, and that ground surrounds Panther Rock.

Chapter One - The Cave

Growing up and living in Anderson County in central Kentucky was truly a wonderful experience. I was surrounded by lakes, rivers, creeks, valleys and everything beautiful nature had to offer. You spent your days as a child not playing with toys, but building forts from branches, and tree houses from limbs. You learned to hunt and fish and you learned the most important lesion of all, nurture the land and the land will be there for you. Do not abuse the land and the land will be there for you. Never take anything you cannot use and let nature take its course. You also learn that everything isn't as it should be. There are times when what should be, isn't. It is during these times when you must step back, look and think. Because what is happening isn't supposed to, it just is. I remember my first trip to Panther Rock. We walked into the field and then we followed a worn path under a large cedar tree. We had to bend over to walk under the tree and when we cleared the tree we were in a circle. The circle seemed out of place, why would this circle be here? As you looked around you could see a rock ledge and then you realized that the ledge was the cutoff point for something. As I walked to the ledge edge I soon saw what the "something" of the cutoff point was. I was looking out at dense woods, hundreds of yards in front of me and I also realized I was standing over one hundred feet above the bottom of the ledge.

A path ran to the right and we walked to this path and saw that it went down and to the left. We slowly eased down the path and headed down to the rocks below. A stream could be seen running calmly through the rocks and as we neared the bottom we saw an opening. The cave is not exceptionally large, yet you feel overwhelmed by the wholeness of the cave due to its structure. The wall cuts back into the rock and you are underneath the wall. Over one hundred feet above your head is solid rock. The woods below the cave are extremely dense and it seems impossible for anything to move through them. As you stand there you have this feeling that you are not alone. It is a feeling that many who go there say they have. It is very quiet in this cave yet at times you feel like something is occurring, something that is not good.

We spent an hour or so just looking around and then we climbed the path back up and started to leave. As we were reaching the top we heard a sound below us, which sounded like a voice had said something in the cave. We just stopped and looked and then continued up. As we walked away I had no idea of what was to come later in my life with regard to this cave. Whether a premonition or a glimpse ahead, that moment always stayed with me and would prove to be a precursor to many events.

In the early 1970's my friend Lee and his dog Rebel and I went to Panther Rock to camp and spend the night. This was nothing new as overnight camping at the cave was common. We built a fire, we explored the area some and we sat and talked as the night descended. Rebel wasn't just any dog, he was part of our group of friends. Rebel and Lee were never apart. If our group of friends went climbing up mountains, this dog went with us. I have seen Lee carry this dog on his back as they climbed up steep rock facings. This dog was just like one of the guys as they say. Rebel was pitch black and was a mixed breed with the build and look of a German Shepherd. As the night moved in we settled down and relaxed around the campfire and then we moved to the ledge overhanging the cave and we sat and talked into the night. The campfire had burned low and I got up to go to my jeep to get a flashlight. When I got up from the rock ledge Rebel got up with me and walked ahead of me as we moved to my jeep. My jeep was parked in the circle in the woods and as I walked past the campfire and in the direction of my jeep, I saw Rebel slow down and start to ease himself down.

He slowly lowered himself, never once taking his eyes off the back right corner of my jeep. I eased my knife out of its sheath and focused my eyes on the same corner. Rebel was not only like one of our group, he was extremely intelligent and fearless. I had seen this dog in many situations with others dogs and he never backed down once. If he had a fault it was his aggressive nature with other dogs. But in all the years around him I had never seen him act like he was acting now. He lowered himself to the ground and growled from deep inside his chest. His ears were laid back and the hair on the nape of his neck was ruffled up. It was like he was moving in slow motion. I was approximately six to eight feet behind Rebel and to his right. The only light was the light from the embers of the campfire and they were enough to give sight to the shadows and the tree line. Rebel was creeping to his right and as I watched him and the right side of the jeep I realized he was trying to see around the back right corner. I could see this area and saw nothing. Rebel eased around and when his line of sight was clear to see the side of the jeep, he then came up slightly off the ground and was staring at the tree line in front of the jeep and to its right. He then lowered quicker than before and I heard him rumble deep in his chest. I looked at the tree line and then I saw something.

I saw a shadow move. It was a humanoid shape and it was moving against the edge of the woods. Whatever this was, Rebel was seeing it, and this fearless dog was afraid of it. This shadow creature or whatever it was, moved with a fluid motion. A motion that was unfamiliar to the eye and the brain. It was like my brain could not rationalize what my eyes were seeing. This shadow moved about 4 feet off the ground and it was like it slipped along the edge of the woods. Then it was gone, just vanished into the darkness of the trees. Rebel then perked up and moved quickly in the direction of the exact spot where the shadow had disappeared. Rebel was acting very strange and was walking back and forth along the edge of the woods, but never going into the woods. Lee had now joined us and I told him briefly what had happened. We all just stood and looked at the woods and then we slowly moved into them. As we entered we heard and saw nothing. Yet there was this feeling that something was around us. Not just in front or behind us, but all around us. Rebel never entered and he remained nervous and restless until we left Panther Rock later that night. Lee did not see the shadow creature. But the dog and I saw it. Perhaps I would have doubted myself if I had been the only witness to this strange event, perhaps the flickering embers and the shadows of the limbs were playing tricks on my eyes and my mind. But this dog saw it clearly, he not only saw it, he was aware of it, and knew where it was located. He also knew something else. Whatever this was it was not something that was to be considered friendly. This shadow that moved in the night was something that possessed coherent thought, it was something that was aware of us, it was something that was watching us, and I got the feeling that it had been there for a very long time.

Panther Rock lures many different types of people to its beauty and mystery. Nature lovers, sightseers, the curious and those who seek the unknown. It is blessed with a botanical wonderland of such a diverse and plentiful amount of wild flowers and plants that many come to just admire the beauty of nature's ground cover. But then again others come to seek what lurks in the darkness and in the cave. Such was the case for three young men who had heard of the cave and decided to go check it out for themselves. These guys were country tough, they feared nothing. They had been in many caves and were not inexperienced in dangerous places. They did not have costly equipment to explore with but instead used what they had, which consisted of rope, a light, brute strength and uncontrolled curiosity.

They arrived at Panther Rock in the middle of the day and made their way down the path and to the cave. Slowly they made their way inside. A short distance from the entry they encountered several holes and decided one of them would be lowered into one to see what could be seen. Two of the men tied the rope securely around their friend and gave him a small light and then carefully lowered him into the hole. Before lowering their friend, they had thrown a rock into the hole and had never heard it hit bottom which provided further encouragement for lowering one member. Slowly the rope slid over the edge of the hole as their friend talked and told them he saw only the walls. Lower and lower he went until they were nearly out of rope and he had to almost yell to be heard. Suddenly there was silence. The two at the top were yelling his name and only heard silence. We walk a thin line between insanity and bravery when events such as this spin out of control. They knew he was still on the rope because they were holding it wrapped around them supporting his weight. All at once the rope jerked several times and they heard screaming. They looked at each other and held tight to the rope. The rope thrashed and it took all their strength to hold on to the rope which held their friend's life in its grasp.

The screaming grew louder and then everything went silent. They yelled their friend's name again and again but received no reply. They began the task of pulling him up without him helping in any way. With their muscles burning as if on fire they pulled and tugged and slowly brought him up. As he came closer he could be heard talking to himself. He was begging them to hurry, to please get him out of this hole. When he finally reached the top and they grabbed him and pulled him onto the rock floor of the cave what they saw left them speechless. Their lifelong friend and buddy was lying on his back and was deathly pale. He was gasping for air and his eyes were fixed and staring up at the cave ceiling. On his face was sweat, but the sweat was unlike anything the two has ever seen. It was huge beads of sweat, so large it looked almost like someone had made pieces of sweat and placed them on his face. The two sat and touched their friend to let him know they were there. As his breathing slowed one of the two asked "What happened down there?" The one who had been lowered into the cave said nothing for a minute or so then he slightly rolled over and quietly said "Get us out of here now, we must go now!" The other two grabbed their friend and helped him out of the cave and helped to carry him up the hill path and to the open area on top. Once there they stopped and the one who had been in the hole laid down on his back. The other two asked again what happened. With a frightened voice he quietly replied "I saw the devil, he is down there, he came out of a side tunnel, I saw him plain as day with my light, I saw the devil, and he is down in that cave."

I had been told this story by one of the two who had been with the man lowered into the hole in the cave. When he told me the story he also told me not to ask the man about what happened because he didn't like to talk about it. Many years passed and one day in a local pool hall I walked in and saw the man standing in the back of the pool room. I had known him for years and had been tempted many times to ask him about this story, but I remembered what his friend had said and had refrained from asking. I cannot say what inspired me at this moment to ask him about the event. As the two of us stood there talking I asked the question, "What did you see in that hole at Panther Rock?" He looked at me and all at once he turned very pale, completely white and pasty looking. Then these huge beads of sweat broke out on his face. He laid his pool stick down and then turned and walked away from me and out the front door of the pool hall. I stood feeling like an idiot and a fool. I could not believe what had just happened and to this day it still makes me feel upset that I asked him the question. He and I have seen each other many times over the years since. But he was never as friendly after that day, he speaks but just moves on and never stops to chat like before. Whatever happened to him down in that hole in Panther Rock changed him forever. Sometimes what lurks in the darkness brings with it eternal change to us all.

A geological "Beauty and the Beast," little known Panther Rock is beautiful to see, but is also heaped in stories and legend that are not for the faint of heart. A Native American chief was mauled to death above the cave in the dead of night by a large black cat, a man swears he saw the devil, and the stories go on and on. But the stories and events do not stop at the cave; they reach out and touch the land that surrounds the cave, and do so with tales that will chill you to the bone.

It was early fall and three friends and I had gone to Panther Rock to enjoy the weather and camp overnight above the cave. We sat around a small campfire and talked till late in the night when we all lay down to sleep. It was almost 3 a.m. when I was suddenly awakened by someone screaming and beating me on the back. Needless to say this was a damn hard way to wake up from a sound sleep and it almost resulted in the other person getting seriously hurt. The person was screaming "Look! Look! Look!" over and over. As I rolled over I saw something out of this world. A bluish, white light was coming from below the ledge and from what appeared to be the mouth of the cave. It was a light like I had never seen before. The others were all sitting on the ground and leaning back as the light shot into the air above the ledge. Sitting and looking at this light was almost hypnotizing. I had never seen a light like this before because there was a strange aspect to it. It was bright yet had a softness to it. It seemed to also be in a ray form yet spread widely. This light shot into the sky yet we could not tell how high. For years stories had been told of strange lights in the area of the cave but I had never heard of any that mentioned a light with this blue color. We all sat silently and just stared. Then as if someone had reached out and flipped a light switch off, the light was gone. It went off so fast I had to think a moment to realize it was gone. The four of us sat and just looked at each other until someone said, "What the hell was that?"

I jumped up and walked quickly to the path that leads down to the cave and I stopped and listened. One thing I then realized was how quiet the woods were. Nothing was moving, not a sound. I walked down the path and to the cave entrance as fast as I could and once there I took my light and looked the area over. Nothing was to be seen anywhere, everything was as peaceful as it could be. There was no way anyone could have left this area and not been heard, it was impossible. And there is no place to hide without making noise. It also seemed impossible to me for anyone to have made this light. I had never before seen a light like this and it would be many years before this odd blue light came to shine on me again.. So what did we see? Perhaps we saw a portal open or a door to another existence? Did something come to Panther Rock that night? Does whatever came through that gateway still roam The Frazier Land?

CHAPTER TWO - THE NEIGHBORHOOD

The land that surrounds Panther Rock is comprised of rolling land-scapes and densely wooded sections with numerous rocky areas. All the land leads to the plateaus of the Kentucky River. The rock in the area is primarily limestone which is conducive to water erosion which results in caves. Several smaller caves can be found in this area known as The Frazier Land but Panther Rock is the largest natural made cave and the most well known in this area. Most of the land owners and especially the ones who have been in the area for many years own large sections of land. From hundreds of acres to even larger tracts, the acreage stretches for miles and miles. Numerous smaller tracts can also be found but the overall area is farm land.

The people who live here are very down to earth, good people. They work hard and enjoy the land and love living in the country. These folks basically keep to themselves and do not meddle in others business. If a neighbor needs help or is in need, the others will be there to help in any way possible. This is just how the people in this area are. One thing we found so interesting was how most of the neighbors knew very little about the other neighbor's stories of strange events. Not every event, but overall the information was not dispersed throughout the area. One man who had lived within 1500 yards of Panther Rock did not even know where it was so had never been to the cave. Others simply acknowledged it was there but never knew of the long history of mysterious tales that are part of the cave. But when you sit down with these folks and you ask about any strange events in the area, well then the stories start to ease out. It takes a little time, effort and understanding, but eventually they come out. They are hesitant to talk as they are all proud people whose names are valuable to them. The world is full of narrow minded people who cannot be opened minded and listen to what good, honest people are saying without allowing their ignorance to open their mouths and ridicule what they are hearing, even though they cannot explain what has happened or what they are hearing. One virtue of all the people in this area is after they get to know you they will sit and talk to you and tell you what they know and have no problem listening to what others think about what they have said or listening when offered a logical explanation of what it could or might have been. But you will find they have no time for nonsense and if someone decides to act foolish and call them names or make derogatory remarks, they just might get what is known as a good old fashioned, country ass kicking.

The people in this area are very self-sufficient and are not known to spend a great deal of time away from their property. They know their land; they walk their land and keep an eye on their land. They also do the same with the farm animals they have and the wild animals who live on their land. This is because the land is special to them. It is not just a piece of dirt, it is their property and everything that exists on their land has meaning to them. This is why when something out of the ordinary is seen or discovered, the people quickly take notice. They are familiar with not only the earth they stand on, but the smells and sounds of the land. What can be found within The Frazier Land is story after story of strange and bizarre events, coming from credible, honest people.

The area around Panther Rock covers many miles and within those miles are many bizarre and unusual stories. Some of these events are from my own personal experiences and some are from others. Very late one night I encountered two of my close friends and they were almost in a state of shock. I had known these two men for many years and I had never seen them in this state of mind. They had been riding in an area known as Gilberts Creek which is within a mile or two of Panther Rock. It was a late summer night and it was warm and they were riding in a small sports car with the top down enjoying the night and enjoying the quiet and tranquility of where they were. The road they were driving on was a single lane rock road which leads to two concrete bridges that crossed over two small creeks which fed the Kentucky River. This area is extremely beautiful and is surrounded by steep cliffs, rock ledges and even waterfalls. But this night something happened that shattered the quiet and tranquility of this natural wonder.

As the two rode along slowly on the rock road they turned a slight curve and entered a short straight area before driving over the first concrete slab. As they turned the curve they both were stunned to see something that made their blood run cold. The driver stopped the car and they both sat frozen in their seats as they watched a creature cross the road in front of them. This creature walked onto the road from a steep cliff. It just walked out into the road in front of them, crossed the road, walked into a field and vanished into the night. They both sat with their hearts pounding and their minds in a frenzy. When someone sees something that defies all they know, it more or less shorts out their logical reasoning and leaves them dazed and confused, which is what was happening to these two men. They then realized that what they saw might decide to come back so the driver took off as fast as he could and drove until he was as far away from this place as he could get.

When these two found me and told me what had happened I was also stunned. What they saw was frightening to even think of, much less be an eyewitness to. The creature they saw was approximately 6 or 7 feet tall. It was walking on its hind legs. It was a canine like creature with what they described as wolf like features. It had the head of a wolf but its stomach was strange looking as it seemed to protrude oddly. Its mouth was gaped open and its front paws were turned down as it walked on its hind legs. It held its arms up and outward. It never turned to look at them, it simply walked across the road, through a ditch and vanished into the night. This is not the only tale of a strange creature with a protruding stomach that walks The Frazier Land, instead it is one of many. What lures all these creatures and events to this area? Does a portal exist that opens and allows creatures from other dimensions to walk among us?

The area called Gilberts Creek is filled with all nature has to offer and is the perfect place for nature lovers to spend time and enjoy the beauty. Whether just sitting by the creek or hiking in the hills, you will be surrounded by all of nature's gifts. My lifelong friend Lee was hiking up a hillside to the right and between the two concrete slabs on the Gilberts

Creek road one day when he and his dog Rebel encountered a very strange cat. They had entered a small open area on the steep hillside when a large deer bolted from their right, bounded across the field and disappeared into the woods. The deer had come from an area where the field ended and a path went across a hillside ledge and back into the cliffs along a creek. Lee watched as his startled dog moved quickly in the direction of the deer then stopped once he realized he was not going to have a chance as it was long gone. Lee smiled at his dog and then watched as he turned in the direction of the ledge path to the right where the deer had come from. Rebel laid his ears back and Lee heard his dog growl deeply. He looked at the area where the path entered the field and what he saw he could not believe.

He was looking at a very large, strange looking, black cat. Lee was not only an experienced outdoorsman, but he was also someone with years of experience dealing with canines and felines in a hands-on environment. He had devoted his life to the care and rescue of all animals and had a sharp eye for detail. The cat he saw was large and he estimated it was over 125 lbs. He told me the cat's head seemed too large for its body and when it turned and moved down the path to leave the area, he saw that the animal moved in what appeared to be an awkward gait. The cat ran slowly with its legs semi-bent and with its stomach hung very low, almost dragging the ground. He said it was very strange to watch it move because it just didn't look like anything he had ever seen before. He also noticed the tail which curled upward numerous times. He said it looked like possibly 4 or 5 circles from the turns of the tail. He said the tail curled up and then forward in circles and the cat held it rather high as it left the area. He said if the cat had straightened out the tail, he would be hard pressed to even guess how long the tail was.

Strange animals, strange sounds, unexplained lights, apparitions, even UFO'S find their way to The Frazier Land. I personally had an event one hot summer day that added the "UFO" factor to the tales of The Frazier Land. I had gone into work early in the afternoon at the rock quarry located in Tyrone, Kentucky. I was to meet my friend, Ray Beasley as he had asked me to work on an antenna and a radio for him. We parked in the middle of the upper section of the quarry in a large open area. His truck was facing west, mine was facing east. I was walking to the passenger door of my truck and was facing east and my friend was walking up behind me. As I opened my truck door I could not move. It was like I was just frozen in place. The dust was whirling around and it was like I was in some kind of vortex. I slowly turned and tried to see my friend. It took all the strength I had to turn slightly but I could just see him out of the corner of my right eye. He was standing with his hand slightly out in front of him and he had a very strange look on his face. I could see his eyes and they showed he was very surprised. He was also in this vortex or whatever had us. The air felt electric and just as suddenly as it started it stopped. I turned to him and asked if he was OK and he just said "What the hell was that?" I could see in his face he was as upset as I was. For some unknown reason I looked up. What inspired me to do so I will never know but when I did my eyes spotted something very far up in the sky. The objects were so far up that it was hard to tell exactly what they were but I could tell there were two of them above us. I kept some binoculars in my truck at all times and I reached in and grabbed them and looked up. Using the binoculars I then had a much better view of the objects above us. They were white and they were perfectly round. They were just sitting in the air and they were not side by side, they were staggered to each other. The first one was positioned to the east with another slightly behind it and to its right. They were so perfectly round it was somewhat hard to think what they were. They were motionless and due to their height in the air it was very hard to gauge their size. I told Ray what I was seeing and handed him the binoculars so he could have a look. He looked and then he handed me the binoculars and said he was leaving. He walked back to his truck, got in and left. I went back to looking at the objects and after about a minute or two they started moving. They moved very slowly at first to the east. They moved in unison and as they moved they gained speed and all at once they seemed to hit a speed that elongated them and they were gone. I walked around my truck and got in and just sat and stared out the window for a long time. Whatever happened to me and my friend that day was something he did not care to discuss. All he ever said was he didn't know what happened and he didn't want to think about it. This happened within just a few miles of Panther Rock and once again, within The Frazier Land. Year after year and time after time, strange and unusual events kept happening, but one event might just be the most unusual of all; maybe even God came to The Frazier Land.

In the late 60's or early 70's I was sitting in a car at a local hangout late one evening. I was a passenger in my friend's car, an early 60's model Ford which had a very large windshield. From where we were sitting we could see a small group of people in the parking lot of the little hamburger business called the Fairgrounds Drive-In, and to our north and slightly west was the local high school. As I was sitting I noticed some lights in the sky over the school, at first I noticed two red lights and then I saw four. As I looked I then noticed the lights were in a diamond formation, the area these covered in the sky was large. I told my friend to check them out and as he did we realized they were moving, also, it appeared that inside the diamond formation you could see the night sky. The diamond formation was elongated, the right and left lights were on the ends of the elongated section with the top and bottom lights shorter in distance apart. The end lights were positioned east and west and the top and bottom lights were north and south, with several degrees either way very possible. At first we were just sitting in his car but as we realized how huge an area the lights covered, we stepped out where we could see without the windshield and any glare affecting our view. The lights were directly over the local high school but were much further toward the distant horizon.

We stood staring at the lights as they began moving, and how strangely they moved, the right light started moving up and the entire formation was rotating, the left light remained stationary. We stepped out of the car and both said nothing, we were transfixed on this formation, several others at the drive-in had also spotted them. We watched as the formation walked end over end across the sky, moving in a south by south east direction. This formation was enormous, from where we were to where it was in the sky was obviously a great distance and this formation covered a large section.

We watched as the formation continued walking through the sky and then disappeared out of our site. We jumped in the car and drove to the road where we knew we could still see it - we only had to drive maybe five hundred yards or so to the bypass. We spotted the formation as it was moving at a steady pace south by south east and then we lost sight of it. We then drove back to the drive-in and the people there were reacting to what they saw, so we got out and talked to them. Several girls were crying and a few guys even jumped in their cars and left. All at once out of the west came two helicopters and a jet, low and moving fast, they were going in the direction of the formation. We stayed at the drive-in restaurant and approximately thirty to forty five minutes later the helicopters and the jet were headed back to where they had come from. The last location that we saw the lights rotating through the sky was in the direction of The Frazier Land. As a matter of fact, they were headed directly for The Frazier Land and from what I found out later, they just might have known exactly where they were headed.

Growing up and living in a rural area one finds himself doing what youngsters do in all rural areas. You ride around, drink, race, chase girls, talk about what men you are, laugh and party. You develop close friendships and you and your friends hang out together and when one is seen it is very likely the others will be seen also. So was the case with a friend of mine. We did all the things I just mentioned and we saw each other daily. My friend lived on the road that led to the area known as Gilberts Creek. He and his family lived back off the road on a cliff side, a very remote location. The day after the sighting of the lights in the sky I did not see him. It was after three or four days that I became concerned and I drove to his house to check on him. This would be a day I would never forget. I drove up to the old farm house and walked to the door and knocked and asked if he was home. I was told yes one moment and that he would come out. I walked to the front of the porch and was standing and thinking what an interesting place this must be to live. All you can see are the woods and hillsides and creeks in the bottoms. As I was standing and looking the area over I heard the door open behind me and my friend walked out. He was someone who smiled all the time, laughed and liked to have fun. He was a good person and never held any ill will toward anyone that I knew of. He also liked to drink and party. When you know someone over a long period of time you grow to understand them and can tell much about them just by looking at the expression on their face, and seeing their eyes.

When I turned I could tell instantly that the person in front of me was not the person I saw the last time I saw my friend.

His eyes looked dead; his face looked tired and old. It was a shock to see him like this. I asked how he was and where he had been, I told him we were all concerned and I then asked if he was alright. He looked at me and said he would not be hanging around with us anymore and that he was now a changed person. I stood a moment and then asked what he meant. He told me that several nights ago he was lying in his bed which was by a window in the upstairs of this old farmhouse. He was looking out the window and as he did he saw these red lights sitting in the sky to the east, he raised the window and looked out and he could see that it was four red lights and they formed a diamond shape and they were rotating end over end but not going anywhere. He then said that a voice told him he must change his ways. He said the voice came from the diamond formation of four red lights. He said the voice was the voice of God and God had told him to change and he had changed. This was one of those moments in life when deciding what to say is rather tough. I stood a moment and then told him ok and I told him to take it easy and I left. I did not tell anyone what he said to me and when asked about him I simply said I had no idea where he was or what he was doing. His life took a turn for the worse after that day. Life was not kind to him and the happy go lucky guy with the endless smile suffered and struggled much through life. This event happened approximately two miles from Panther Rock and right in the middle of The Frazier Land.

Mysteries within mysteries can be the most mysterious of all. And what you are about to read is a true mystery within several mysteries. Near the top of the path that leads down to the cave at Panther Rock is a large tree. The exact type of tree is unknown at this time. One day Darrel Gabhart walked over near the tree and noticed something odd. On the ground around the tree were a large number of pieces of small branches. These pieces were scattered all around the tree.

This was not just one or two pieces, but a very large number of them. Darrel paused and studied the pieces in his hand and looked over the

area. He looked up into the tree and could see that something had taken these small branches from the tree's outside edges. Some might say that this was easily explained as it was a squirrel or some kind of bird. Others have stated it might be some kind of insect. The only problem with all these ideas is they are wrong. These pieces of branches are not just random pieces. The pieces are very similar in size. Each piece has an angle cut on the ends. These angle cuts are extremely close to being the same angle. But what makes this so mysterious is the fact that these branches are split down the middle with a precision that is hard to even begin to explain. No animal, bird or insect can split these small branches with the precision that they were cut. And as stated earlier, this was not just a branch or two scattered here and there, this was what was described as several pickup truck beds full of these pieces.

Animals can do some amazing things, but to take these small twigs and split them with the consistency and precision they are cut with is beyond explanation. Those who have seen the pieces and examined them all say the same thing, and that is, we have no idea what could have done this. Seasoned outdoorsmen and farmers and those who have spent their lives in the outdoors are baffled. The tree itself is approximately 70 feet tall and sits on a ledge overlooking the area formed by water running out of the Panther Rock cave. Discussions have raged on about this mystery and to this day no one has an answer. These wood pieces are scattered all around and were taken from the outside of this tree. Every area of the tree had these pieces removed. What reason could there be for something doing this? One idea was that something was eating the center pulp out of these little twigs. However it must be assumed that whatever was doing this must have been starving or insane to get food in this way. The time it would take to cut off each section and then split the small section and then eat the tiny amount of core would make it seem very unlikely this was done to acquire food. Also discussed was where the splitting was done? Was it done in the air or in the tree or on the ground? What could hold these small pieces and cut them at these almost precise angles and then split them down the middle with such precision? Adding to the mystery is the fact that now it seems the tree is dying or at least a section of the tree is dying. No answers, only questions, another mystery in The Frazier Land, and this mystery overlooks the cave known as Panther Rock.

Near Panther Rock is an underpass that is known as Graffiti Tunnel. This underpass has the Bluegrass Parkway running over it and over the years the young scoundrels have covered the walls of the tunnel with layer upon layer of graffiti. But according to many there is something that doesn't like people being in the tunnel at twelve o'clock at night. If there is no traffic on the tunnel road or the parkway, at exactly twelve p.m. you can hear something coming down off the parkway and through the grass and then you can hear it slowly walking inside the tunnel. What it's looking for or what it's doing no one knows, but it has been heard numerous times over the years.

What of the strange stone squares which can be found no more than a mile or two from Panther Rock near the cliffs of the Kentucky River. These huge, perfectly cut, stone squares are just laying in a field and as to who put them there and why remains a mystery. Also at one time a large circular stone could be seen which had hieroglyphic type markings on it. The large circular stone lay on a hillside and over the years the weather and age took the markings from it. But I saw those markings and without a doubt they looked like ancient symbolism. Also the stories of old tombstones that have strange demonic writings on them or the stories of the lights that float through the valley of Gilberts Creek and can be seen from the cliff tops across the Kentucky River and seen from the Woodford County side. One fact about The Frazier Land that should be considered is that just because the Kentucky River flows through the land does not necessarily mean the river banks are any kind of border for The Frazier Land. I am of the opinion that The Frazier Land runs into Woodford County which is across the river and to the east. There are many stories about The Frazier Land that I cannot write about due to promises made and for the safety of others and also to protect the natural tranquility and beauty of certain areas. The Native American presence in Kentucky is well documented as is the Native American presence in The Frazier Land. But to those who know the area and the lay of the land, the events from past times are still to be found in different ways. I know of holes in the ground where buckets full of Native American artifacts can be brought out any time. This area is within just a few miles of Panther Rock but unless someone knows where to look, the odds of someone finding it are very slim. Due to the huge number of artifacts in these holes as well as other specifics, I have always been under the impression that The Frazier Land was a meeting place. I once had an old one tell me that was true, the area around Panther Rock and the surrounding area was a special place to the Native Americans. The land in this area held great powers and was used for meetings between tribes and the meetings took place high on certain hills overlooking the valleys below. I have always wondered what occurred that made the Native Americans dump their precious goods into these holes in the earth. Were they offerings to a spirit? Where they given as part of a ceremonial practice? Were the Native Americans trying to appease something that moved in the night, something older than time? Something they encountered yet were unable to understand and they could only hope by making offerings that whatever this was it would let them hunt and exist in peace.

Many years ago a man and his young nephew were walking along a creek near the area where the two large square white colored rocks are laying on the ground. As they walked along the tree line near the top of the creek bank they realized they were not alone. When they would move, something in the creek would move with them, when they would stop, whatever was pacing them would stop. Both were armed and both had their weapons ready in case they were needed. This strange movement with them continued and in their minds it was not a person. They felt sure it was a large animal by the sounds it made when it moved. One thing they felt certain of was that whatever this was, it was walking upright and was heavy. They were experienced outdoorsmen and knew the sounds of movement made by four legged and two legged creatures. The one person who told me of this also told me of a feeling. A feeling of being watched. But he also said for some reason the feeling made him think of olden times, as if whatever this was had lived through the ages. He said he knew that sounded crazy but that is how it made him feel. Unknown to this man was the fact he was surrounded by ancient history. He was in a remote part of The Frazier Land where not only the two large square stones lay, but he was near the large round stone with the ancient symbols on it. He was also near an area where at some time a massacre had occurred, as well as the area where tombstones can be found that have strange wording that speaks of evil.

On and on the stories go, stories that are told over and over. The stories I am writing about in this book are just the ones I have knowledge of. I cannot even begin to imagine the number that are known by others, and kept quiet. Most events of this nature remain silent. Most people, for various reasons just keep these types of events to themselves. But one thing is for certain, within The Frazier Land and all around Panther Rock, the number of unexplained, strange and unusual events far exceeds what might be considered an average amount of unnatural events.

CHAPTER THREE - THE X FARMER

The individual known as The X Farmer has chosen to remain anonymous and his request to do so will be honored in this book and on the DVD.

He loved the land he had bought; he planned to raise his family there and enjoy life with his family. Over 100 acres and it was his, he would build a home by hand, he would carry rocks from the river banks and they would be laid with care. But as he worked his mind always drifted back to that night when he was camping on his new property, before anything had been built. He remembered lying by his camp fire in 1977 thinking of the future and of having a family. He thought how quiet the night sky looked and how this was where he wanted to be. But his tranquility was broken when he suddenly heard large limbs cracking. He could hear something moving, he could hear the thump of a heavy foot as it hit the ground. He sat up and looked in the direction of the sounds. He had spent much of his life in the outdoors and he could sense that something was out there, and it was something different and he also felt it was something he could not control, something the pistol in his hand might not stop.

He got up and left his campsite and left his property for the time being. He never forgot this night, it stayed in his memory, and it stayed as a reminder, a reminder of what was to come.

He did as he promised and built the house by hand; he carried rocks on wagons from the river shores and placed them with care. He would stop from time to time and just look around and smile, this was his land, and he owned it. As he looked around he never knew that within 1500 yards of his property was a cave that held many stories, and many mysteries, a cave known as Panther Rock. Sometimes he would work late as he steadfastly built his house; he would be building as the night fell on the land. At times he would stop and listen as he would hear sounds that he wasn't familiar with. In time his father came to stay on his land, living in a small trailer near the house. One day his father asked if his son had a gun he could keep in the trailer. The X Farmer asked his father why he needed a gun and his father told him it was just to have with him as he had no weapon in the trailer other than a hammer. The son knew his father well and wondered why he wanted a gun so he asked if his father had seen something that made him want a weapon. His father said he had not seen anything but he was hearing sounds that made him uneasy and he would feel much better at night if he had a weapon with him. His father told him the sounds come late at night mostly around the time the cool damp comes. The X Farmer looked at his dad and asked what he was talking about, what was the cool damp? His dad then explained to his son what the cool damp was. Just before midnight he told his son the air would change and this happened often. As the hour approached midnight the air temperature changed and a slight breeze carried this cool damp feeling air down through the low lying areas of the land. He told his son it was about this same time he would hear sounds he was not familiar with and at times it almost sounded like the sounds were riding on the cool damp. The X Farmer got his dad an old 22 he had in his house and gave it to him. The X Farmer never forgot what his dad told him and as time rolled on he also knew what it felt like to be touched by the cool damp. Perhaps the cool damp was more than just a temperature change as day became night, perhaps the air turning cool as it moved through the lowlands was not just some natural occurrence, maybe it was a door opening, maybe it was the way for things of a paranormal existence to walk into our reality?

In 1984 The X Farmer and his close friend were inside a shed preparing to work on the house The X Farmer was building. As they gathered their tools they heard loud sounds coming from outside. They both listened intently as the sounds moved through the brush outside and in the direction of the creek down the hill. They both stood quiet and listened as whatever was moving through the brush outside broke limbs and made strange sounds as it moved along. The X Farmer moved to the door and slowly stepped out to look over the area. As he scanned the land he saw nothing and noticed the sounds had stopped, then his eyes caught something. There was something in the rafters of the house he was building. At first he could not tell what his eyes were seeing. But soon his eyes focused and he realized he was seeing what appeared to be a huge owl. The owl was so big it was hard to imagine it was real. He stood and whispered to his friend to come look. As his friend moved out the door and The X Farmer turned back to look at the house, the bird, or whatever it was, was gone. He stood and looked at the empty area where the huge bird had been. His mind wondered what he had seen. Was what he had seen a huge bird? Or was it something else? What made those noises? How was whatever made the noises connected to the bird? Or was the bird just something he was supposed to think he saw? Had The X Farmer just seen a Shape Shifter?

He worked on his land and house on and off for several years and was finally able to move in and get settled around 1986. One night he and his young son heard something that brought them both to a standstill. As they were outside and getting ready to go back in the house suddenly a scream rushed through the night. They both stopped and turned and looked in the direction of the scream. The scream sounded like it was coming from the back of the property. Neither of them had ever heard a scream like this one, there was something hollow and almost evil to this sound. It was a sound that did not bring to mind any animal they knew of, it only brought thoughts of confusion and the unknown to them both. The next morning The X Farmer got his gun and walked back in the direction of where he thought the sound might possibly have come from. He walked through dense brush into an area he had not been in a lot and as he entered a semi-open space he stopped because something was not right. It took him a minute or two for his mind to translate what he was seeing, which was a large number of trees broken off and the tops on the ground. They were all broken off at approximately 7 feet up from the ground. All these trees were about 3 to 4 inches in diameter. He entered the area and looked closely at the damage. There were no signs of anything other than the broken off trees. The X Farmer guessed there were between 30 to 50 trees broken off, they had not been cut off, they were definitely broken off because none were hanging, they were all on the ground. What could have done this? How could it have been done? Something had to reach up at least 6 or 7 feet from the ground and then grab these trees and snap them off. Or did something climb into the trees and break them off?

He stood perplexed and bewildered. His mind raced as he realized if there was a creature on his land that could reach up and snap off a tree in this manner then he was in danger. He then thought how one tree would be a task to break, but how in the world could something do that to upwards of 50 trees? The trees were freshly broken, and the tops were not all laying in the same direction, they were laying in random patterns. No storms had occurred in many days, especially not the night before. As The X Farmer walked around he looked for tracks and signs of any kind that would be a clue as to what had happened. He saw absolutely nothing, no tracks, no signs of anything, only broken off trees. He walked out of the area and to this day has no idea what happened, what made that scream and why or how those trees were broken off.

The X Farmer owns over one hundred acres of land and much of his property is hard to move through. The trees and underbrush have grown thick forming an impassable barrier in many areas. The X Farmer at times has cut his way into these areas not for need of the land, but out of curiosity. It was while cutting his way into a dense section of his land that he made a discovery. He had spent several days cutting his way into a densely grown area, it was hard work and cutting through the thick growth with a machete was back breaking. He had made his way deep into an area when he found himself in an opening. He walked out into this opening and looked around. As he did he realized he was standing in a circle. He looked around the area intently. He looked at the ground which had grass growing but no thick cover like all the other areas. He looked at the trees around the circle. What he was seeing did not make sense to him. Why would this circle be here? Had someone done something to make the circle? He walked the edge of it and looked for entrance paths, but he could not find any. If something had been built here years ago then why had the trees and brush not regrown? He looked up at the tops of the trees around the circle and saw no evidence of burn marks or scaring. He spent a great deal of time examining the circle and the land around the circle, and he was as clueless as to what had created it when he left the area, as he was when he arrived. An interesting aspect to the circle is the fact that another one exists at Panther Rock above the ledge where you can look out over the cave below. This circle has been in this location for as long as anyone can remember.

Cairns are artificial piles of rocks. These piles of rocks can be found world-wide and date back to ancient times. The use of these stacks or formations of rocks are varied. They can be trail markers and burial markers, they can hold special religious meanings, they can mark boundary lines, and some are even placed at times to keep the dead from rising. They can also take the form of animals or manlike structures.

The X Farmer was cutting his way through some very dense brush on his land one day when his eye caught something standing in the woods. At first he thought it was a huge creature of some sort, or maybe a very large person standing in the woods. As he looked closer he realized

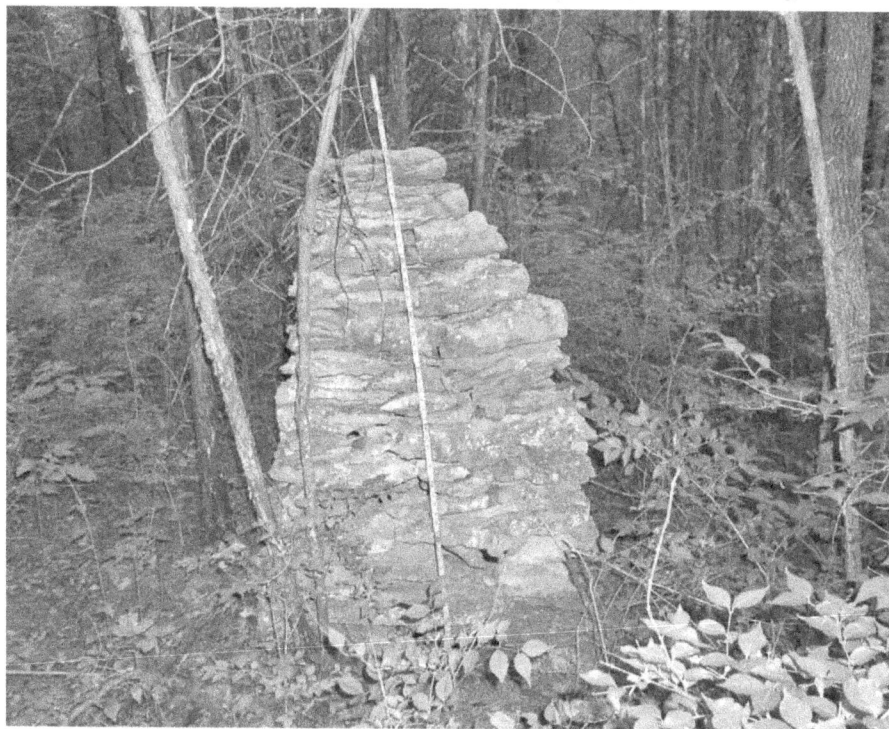

he was looking at a pile of stones, but not just any pile of stones. These rocks were placed with purpose to form a structure. This structure was over 6 feet tall and somewhat symmetrical. He looked through the dense brush and moved forward toward the structure. As he approached, his mind was racing as he wondered who had built it and why? What did it mean and why was it here?

He moved around the structure and examined it closely. He could see that the builder had tried to make a four sided structure from the rocks. He could see that each stone was laid with purpose; they were not placed without meaning and planning. This was not some random pile of rock. Someone had taken time and effort to build this. He spent many minutes examining the cairn and then he moved in close to see if this stack had anything inside. The top was of great interest to him as it appeared two flat rocks had been placed on top and each of these rocks had a very unique characteristic. They appeared to have semicircular holes which had been made by water. These semi-round holes looked exactly like where water had run or dripped over a very long period of time and eventually made a hole in the rock. The two top stones were opposing each other, with the semi-round holes facing each other. It is hard to say if they had been one rock originally. The center of this large Cairn was hollow and it appears the designer had that in mind when it was built.

The X Farmer stepped back and stared for a few minutes at this odd structure, then decided to look around and see if any more of these were in this area. This section of his property is almost impenetrable. The trees and brush had grown for hundreds, if not thousands, of years collectively and the thorns on some of the trees were up to three inches in length. Small trees filled the voids below the large trees thus making a dense wall which was very hard to see through and extremely hard to walk through. As The X Farmer slowly cut and moved through this natural barrier he suddenly stopped and saw another rock cairn. This one was smaller than the first but of the same construction method. As the years rolled on, he would find numerous cairns of various sizes and several strange rock structures including some flat rocks that formed a shape on the ground but seem to be connected to nothing. Why are these structures located where they are? The area where these cairns are located would not seem to be land that anyone would live on or have much use for as this area is on a steep hillside. What do they mean? Who built them? These questions remain unanswered and may remain that way. However it is rather ironic that these strange rock structures are located within less than a half mile from Panther Rock.

In 1988 The X Farmer had put in a long day of work and was preparing to retire for the evening when he heard something out in the front of his house. At first he wasn't sure exactly what was occurring but as he walked out the door it became apparent that something serious was taking place. He had 3 dogs, all mixed breeds and each weighing somewhere in the neighborhood of 60 to 70 lbs. Two of the dogs looked very much like Dobermans and the third one was larger by about 10 lbs. All three dogs were farm dogs, they roamed freely so the entire farm was their home and their territory. These dogs were very self-sufficient and capable of taking care of themselves in the outdoors. As The X Farmer walked out his door he grabbed a small flashlight and proceeded to make his way to the front of his house which faced up a slight grade, so he could see what was happening with his dogs.

It was obvious from the sounds that the dogs were in a terrible fight; the sounds he heard were different from anything he had ever heard his dogs engage in before. As he moved to a position where he could shine his light and get a good look at what the dogs were fighting, he realized the fight was near the top of his lot where the open area of his yard merged with the tree line of the woods where the road to his home ran through. He shone his light as he positioned himself but the light was not bright enough to fully illuminate the area of the fight due to the distance. But what he could see stunned and mystified him. He could see his dogs rushing an animal of some kind, but his mind could not identify it. Whatever this animal was it reminded him of an enormous sheep dog, because it was four legged and had a matted grayish colored coat. This animal's stomach seemed to be very low to the ground, and as the dogs would rush in and attack this creature The X Farmer would see it swat the dogs with its front paws and slap them so hard they rolled away. The dogs were yelping and screaming as they kept attacking it. The X Farmer estimated the creature was between 100 and 150 pounds. The fight between the creature and the dogs then moved into the tree line and into the woods. The X Farmer stood and listened as the fight raged on. He thought of getting a gun and going to try and stop the fight but as it was dark and he wasn't sure what the animal was and he felt his dogs could take care of themselves, he turned and went back into the house and prepared for bed. As he stood in his kitchen he froze in his tracks as he realized something that made no sense to him. At no time had he heard any sounds other than those from his dogs, not one sound from the other animal, nothing. He stood a moment and turned and looked back at the door and thought about looking out one more time, but decided as he was exhausted he would just go to bed and in the morning he would go out and see if he could find anything that might give a clue as to what this animal was.

The next morning he awoke and after a quick breakfast he walked outside to look over the area where the fight had occurred and check on his dogs. He called his dogs as he walked out the door but this time they did not appear as they always did. He called them again with no response. He then walked out into his yard and this time he yelled loudly for them. He stopped and listened and heard a slight whimper from around the side of the house. He walked around and saw two of his dogs laying in the yard. Both dogs were lying on their sides and were badly hurt. He rushed to them and started looking them over. They seemed to be suffering from the same type of wounds. The claws had cut deep into the dog's faces and resulted in gaping wounds. He decided to take the dogs to the vet but it was then he realized he had a dog missing. He began looking for the larger mixed breed dog. He rushed around looking for it and calling but didn't see him and got no response. The missing dog was never seen again. Although a thorough search was performed, no sign what-so-ever was found. The area where the fight took place was examined closely for tracks or anything else that might give a clue as to what this creature was, but nothing was found. The X Farmer concluded that whatever this creature was, it killed and carried off a tough 70 lb. farm dog.

The Frazier Sound Can Be Heard On the DVD.

In 1995 The X Farmer was back on his land cutting timber. He had stopped to take a break and was sitting on a stump drinking water from a pint jar he kept with him when outdoors. As he leaned his head back to take a drink he heard something. He did not move, but stayed in position. He had spent his life in the outdoors and had heard every sound that could be made in this part of Kentucky. At first he wasn't sure what he was hearing, this sound was something new to him. The sound was like a scream and a howl mixed. As for what type of creature was making this sound he had no idea. But he sat and listened as the creature made its sound a few times then fell silent. He stood up and looked around the land where he was standing and wondered what the hell he had just heard. Over the years he heard the sound many times, sometime at a distance and sometimes close by, too close.

One afternoon he was in a densely wooded area of his property when he heard the sound. It was no more than 50 feet away from him. He stood and raised his gun and pointed it in the direction of the sound. The sound then came toward him. This made The X Farmer extremely nervous because he was not sure what kind of animal would move toward a man. This sound was loud enough to lead a person to believe it was being made by a large animal, as to how large, that would be hard to say, but in The X Farmer's mind, this was a very large animal. He stood with his gun pointed and waited, waiting for whatever this was to come through the brush and make itself seen. The sound stopped and never started again. He stood and listened and waited. He heard nothing, no sounds, no limbs moving, he did not hear the sounds of an animal moving through the woods and this area was extremely dense almost impossible to move through. He lowered his gun and took a deep breath and wondered to himself what had made this sound and was it still there? Was it watching him? This would not be his last en-counter with The Frazier Sound, far from it - this would be just one of many.

Over the years he and his family and even his friends heard the sound. It was in 2007 that I sent a recording device to The X Farmer. It was

4:10 a.m. on November 7th, 2007 and The X Farmer was standing in his kitchen when he heard the sound outside. He grabbed the small digital recording device and microphone and walked out on his porch and recorded The Frazier Sound. The X Farmer was standing in a position where his log house was between him and the sound. He estimated that the sound was coming from a creek bed which was 150 feet from his house. So this makes this recording over 150 feet away with a large house between the recording device and the sound. Many have listened to the recording, many highly experienced outdoor people and they all say the same thing, they have never heard anything like this sound. Outdoorsmen with over 50 years of experience, hunters and trackers and those who have lived in the outdoors all their lives all say the same, they have never heard anything like this sound and have no idea what made it. Individuals such as Pennsylvania resident Dana Scouten who is a retired law enforcement officer. Dana Scouten has spent his entire life as a hunter and outdoorsman. Traveling to the mountains of the western U.S. and into the wilderness of Canada and along the eastern states fishing and hunting. He has over 50 years of outdoor experience and after listening closely to The Frazier Sound he says he has never heard anything like it and has no idea what made this sound.

Another strange aspect of this sound is that the farm dogs will not go after whatever is making the sounds. These are outdoor dogs which interact with every animal in the area. These dogs are not shy about protecting what they consider their area and they consider their area anywhere on The X Farmer's land. The dogs will take notice of the sound at times, but at other times it is as if they do not know the sound is occurring. At times they look in the direction of the sound or even move in the direction of the sound but at no time will they enter the woods to engage whatever is making it.

The recording must be listened to closely, very closely. For as everyone focuses on the main sound there is something else happening. When you listen to The Frazier Sound you must listen to the background sounds and in between the sounds. Listen very closely and you will be very surprised at what you hear.

I have known The X Farmer for many years and when I moved away from Lawrenceburg and Anderson County he and I stayed in touch through emails and phones calls. Both of us were busy with the daily trials of life and sometimes we would go for long periods of time without contacting each other. One day in a phone conversation The X Farmer and I were discussing the area around where he lived and I had told him of the Panther Rock cave and that many mysterious things have occurred over the years in his area. He then told me he had a picture of a very strange animal track. He said he had been having some work done on a creek behind his house and a man had been digging with a small piece of equipment and widening an area of the creek for him. One morning in 2002 he walked back to where the work was taking place and he noticed in the fresh mud a large animal track. This track was unusual in several regards. He realized he needed to not only get a picture of this track but to also get something to measure it with and if possible, to get a witness. He accomplished all three by taking several pictures, laying a Lufkin ruler down by the track for measurement reference and bringing his friend to see the track for himself. I asked him if he had the picture and if I could see it. He said he would look for it and if he found it he would send the picture to me. Finding the picture turned into a real odyssey for The X Farmer but his lovely wife found it, had it scanned and then emailed to me. At first glance this track appeared to be that of a large cat, but once I examined and analyzed it carefully, I realized this was not a cat (feline) track. One would logically conclude that for a track to have the symmetry and appearance this track did, that the only other explanation would be canine. But upon closer examination I determined this was not a canine track.

Feline and canine tracks have some similarities; however, there are very precise and distinct differences in the tracks made by these animals. One aspect of this track that added great mystery to finding its creator was the size of it which was much bigger than any mountain lion track that I know of. Upon speaking with numerous experts and outdoorsmen and showing them this photo they all agreed on one thing, whatever made it was a very large animal. The general consensus from the feline crowd was that it was most likely a very large dog; the track was

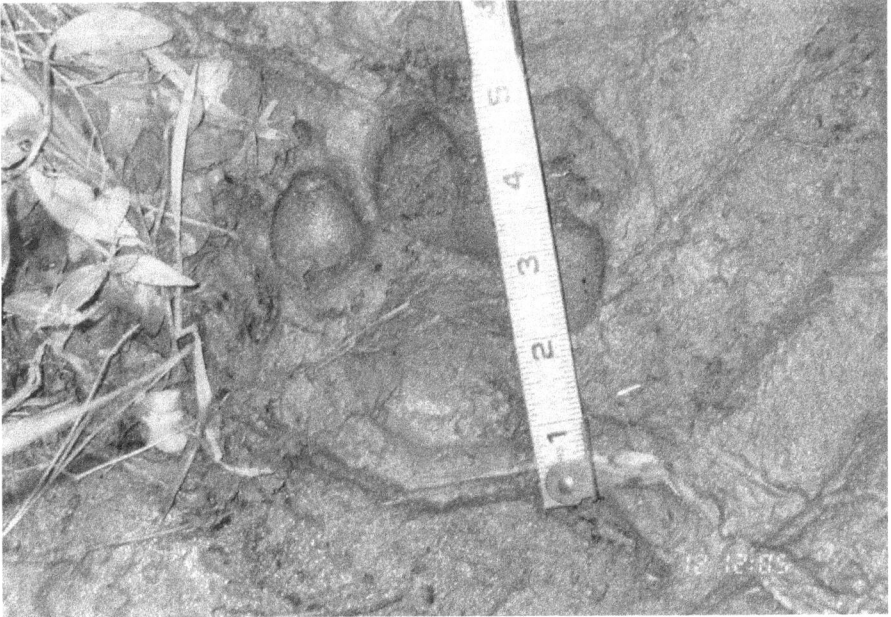

just too big to be a feline track as a very large mountain lion will only throw a track of 3.5 inches. So due to this and other reasons, this must be a canine track. The canine folks said this must be a feline track. It could not be a canine track as they have certain specific characteristics that definitely separate them from a feline track and several of these specifics were not in place making this most definitely feline. I laughed to myself as I received replies from both camps as they were basically saying the same thing, although in a very roundabout way, they never actually knew what made it. There are a few things that are known about this track which is now known as The Frazier Mud Track. This track was made by a large animal and due to the size and depth of the track impression, this animal/creature obviously carried weight. The animal had toenails/claws and was most likely a predator of some type. As only one track was found other aspects of the animal's size would be pure speculation. But what happened near the location where the track was found on The X Farmer's land were events that didn't need much speculation at all.

Within a week of The Frazier Mud Track being found a terrible event happened nearby. On a farm no more than a mile away from where the track was found something wicked happened to a cow. One day the man and woman who owned a farm near The X Farmer were going about their daily routines. Suddenly the woman heard a crashing sound out back. She ran outside and saw that one of their cows that was kept in a back field had crashed through the back gate and was in the yard. As she stood and looked at the cow she noticed something was wrong. She moved closer and saw that the cow was seriously injured. Both the cow's ears were torn completely off down to the skull and the cow's right eye was torn out. The cow's back had deep cuts where something had dug its claws into it. The local vet was called and with hard work he managed to save the cow. This cow lived for many years and pictures were taken to show what happened to it. Although it was tried in vain to obtain the pictures, they could not be found to show in this book or the DVD. I personally spoke with this couple and they are down to earth, hard working, honest people. Whatever happened to their cow no one will ever be able to say for certain, but what is for certain is that whatever did this was very powerful. This cow was a 700 lb. adult, not a calf. Also in this same time period on a farm nearby, several horses were attacked in almost the same fashion. Something was roaming The Frazier Land and whatever it was, it had a taste for blood and had no qualms about attacking large farm animals to get it.

I decided to send The X Farmer some recording equipment and also a trail camera to place on the property and see if we could capture any audio or video evidence. The X Farmer was diligent in his work with the trail cam over the months and would move it from location to location over time. Several images were captured that we just cannot be sure of. One looks like a bear, possibly a bear, the image is not especially clear but by enlarging it and running it through multiple filters it certainly seems like it might be a bear. One thing is for certain, whatever this animal is, it is large, over one hundred pounds. Another image captured is even stranger. At first when I received the image from The X Farmer I thought I was seeing a dog standing sideways with its head turned to the left staring at the camera. However upon closer examination I realized that what I thought was the dog's tail and back legs was neither. They were branches on a nearby tree. We captured many images of deer and even a person every now and then. One shot showed a light floating in the air. Overall nothing conclusive was captured but we did get several very interesting images which can be seen on the DVD or will be posted on my website: philipspencer.net.

The area where the cairns are located covers between 10 to 12 acres of land and as stated before this land is extremely hard to traverse. In 2004 The X Farmer made another discovery. He decided to cut a path into a section of his land to open the area up more. He used heavy equipment and backbreaking hand work to accomplish this project. As he worked his way down a steep sloping hillside he came upon another mystery. He found a rock fence with an opening. And at the opening in the rock wall he saw something he had never seen before. Lying on the ground was a rock. A rather large rock and it was split in half. This rock was not the type you would find in this area of his land. This was a river stone that someone had carried to this area and placed where it laid. The split stone was pointing toward an opening in the rock wall and the opening was located between two very old, large trees. The X Farmer examined the split stone closely and it was his opinion that the splitting of this stone was not done naturally, instead it was done by someone intentionally.

Split stones and their purposes are quite subjective. The reasons for and uses of split stones are very diverse and greatly discussed. Some split stones are considered markers, or pointers to show the way. What these split stones point the way to can be varied but in many cases it is considered a ceremonial marker. Split stones can also be found in areas where portals to the underworld are thought to exist. They might point the way to these portals or they might point the way out for whatever comes through the portal from the underworld. Is the split stone a clue to the strange events of the area? Does it mark or point the way to a portal? What does or did the stone fence surround? What part in this entire aspect of The Frazier Land do the cairns play as they are in the area surrounded by the ancient stone walls?

In 2006 The X Farmer's son was out on the porch late one night talking to his girlfriend on his cell phone. Lost in a young man's dreams and fancies he stood leaning on a support post talking about things only those who are young and in love talk about. Suddenly the tranquility of a perfect night and conversation was broken by a scream. This was not just any scream, it pieced right to the soul. The young man jerked and looked in the direction the scream had come from. He was then jarred a second time when the scream came again. Although his location was a long distance from the area of this scream, the sound was so loud and intense that it seemed to be all around him. He closed his phone and turned and walked into the house. He went to his room and sat on his bed and looked at the wall. This event changed things on The X Farmer's land. Up until this time the young folks had camped and partied on the back of the property. The X Farmer's sons would have their friends over and they would have cookouts and camp overnight. This all came to a halt when the older son heard this scream. No more campouts. No more cookouts. No more friends over to spend the night camping under the stars.

The son concluded that what he had heard must be a large cat. And not just a large domestic cat, not just a large wild cat, this scream could only have been made by an extremely large cat. A cat along the lines of a cougar or another large cat of that type. What other animal could make this kind of scream? As with other events on The X Farmer's land

and within The Frazier Land people can only choose an explanation that is available to common knowledge. They will choose what it might be as opposed to what it actually is because what it actually is, is unknown.

In 2007 The X Farmer and his wife were sitting on the porch relaxing after a long day and discussing the day's events. His wife decided to head inside and go to bed. The X Farmer sat on the porch in his old rocking chair and listened to the sounds of the night, crickets chirping, a bird making a sound every now and then, a dog barking in the distance, and even far away the sound of a lone car or truck was moving along a road somewhere. As he sat he realized everything had become very quiet. Everything had not only become quiet but it had become a little too quiet. He eased up in his chair and listened intently for any sounds that might tell him why everything else had gone silent. As he sat he heard something move in a creek approximately 150 feet from his porch. He could hear large limbs being moved or stepped on. He could tell from the heavy sounds they made that something was stepping on them or moving them and letting them hit the ground. He then heard something that chilled him. He heard deep breathing, not really labored breathing, but deep breathing. This breathing sounded like it was coming from something very large. It did not sound like the breathing of a person or any animal he had ever heard in the outdoors. There was something very different about this sound.

The X Farmer sat and listened as whatever this was made its way down the creek then moved out of hearing distance. He eased up from his chair and went inside and picked up a shotgun and walked back outside. This was more a ceremonial move as he was sure whatever this was had moved on, but he stood on his porch in the dark and listened and watched for a while. He soon turned and went back inside and retired for the night. The next morning as soon as the chores were done he went directly to the area of the creek where he had heard the sound the night before. It had rained slightly and the ground was wet enough to capture a good track so he had high hopes that whatever had moved through the night before making those sounds had also left some tracks. He looked in the area of least resistance where he thought something might have moved through. It was in the third such section that he saw something on the ground, and realized he was looking at a huge footprint. He stopped and looked closely and became extremely excited. He turned and quickly went back to his house and picked up his phone and called me. When he told me what he had found I asked him if he had marked the place where the tracks were. He replied no, he got so excited he forgot to mark the exact location but he said he felt sure he could find it. I told him to hang up the phone immediately, grab a camera and a measuring device and go straight to the spot and take pictures and measurements and if he had anything to make a cast of the tracks to do so. He hung up and did as I had instructed him to do.

When he returned to the area he could not find the original track which he said was much more distinctive than the two he took pictures of. The track he photographed is of a right foot. The foot measures from tip of heel to tip of large toe approximately 20 inches. The pictures are not the best for showing the track even though the ground was muddy; the ground was also covered with leaves and just did not take the imprint as well as we hoped it would. However, I had The X Farmer draw an outline of the foot as he saw it and superimpose his outline over the actual photo of the foot. The large toe is a point of interest. From his outline he thinks the creature slipped and this is the toe imprint showing slippage and that explains the odd enormity of the big toe imprint. In his outline he also drew inwards in the area of the arch. He said he thought the creature was leaning or doing something that made it rise off the arch and dig the big toe into the mud resulting in the extended looking big toe. As anyone can see this is an enormous track. With all the strange events surrounding Panther Rock we now add this huge foot print to the collection. This track was within 1500 yards of Panther Rock. The enormity of this track is only superseded by the enormity of the number of bizarre and strange events near this cave. For the sake of clarity I outlined the footprint with a thick gray color to show the outline of the foot better as The X Farmer drew very small red dots in his outline. The X Farmer was sent my outline and approved the overlay I had done.

The X Farmer often sits and rocks in his chair and thinks about all the events on his land that he just cannot explain. He thinks of why his land is the place for all this to occur. Perhaps it is not his land that draws the unexplained to it, but perhaps all the events take place because of something that happened to The X Farmer when he was a young boy. In 1958 The X Farmer lived just a few miles from Panther Rock in Woodford County which is east, across the Kentucky River from Anderson County. He and a friend were doing what they did every day, what young boys do out in the countryside of Kentucky. Walking back through the hills, creeks and fields while talking and passing the day away. However, this day would be like none before it. As they were walking through a field with numerous large trees in it The X Farmer felt like he was being watched. When you grow up in the outdoors you develop senses that others do not have. You develop these because you need them to survive. These senses are actually not something unnatural to humans, they are part of each and every one of us but we have let them dissolve over the years by being distracted by an information/technology based society that is only causing us to drift further away from our true selves and our place in nature. The X Farmer stopped walking and as he did his friend stopped also. It was then The X Farmer looked up. What he saw did not register with his mind at first. Sitting no more than ten or fifteen feet above a large tree was an oblong metallic craft. It sat motionless and soundless. The X Farmer said to his friend "look up there," and as he did he pointed to the object. As they both stood and stared at it they were speechless. The object appeared to be a metallic craft but the metal was not shiny it was dull in color. The craft was approximately thirty feet long and maybe six feet wide. The two boys stood staring into the sky at this silent anomaly. The boys were no more than one hundred feet from the craft. This sighting lasted between five and ten minutes. After a few minutes the boys moved and as they walked they never took their eyes off the craft. It was hard for them to tell if the craft moved but they seemed to think it did follow them as they slowly moved along. The entire time they were engaged with this craft they felt like they were being watched. Not only did they feel like they were being watched, they felt it intensely. At one time they felt like they were within fifteen or twenty feet of the craft on the ground with it being thirty to forty feet above them in the air. The boys stated they never were directly under the craft, but felt as if once they moved they were much closer to it than they were when they first saw it.

Suddenly they saw the craft rotate and slowly start moving straight up. As it did it gained speed and then in the blink of an eye, it was gone. They boys were absolutely certain this was not a balloon or any type of craft from this planet. The X Farmer said he and his friend turned and walked away and headed back to their homes and very seldom spoke about what they had seen that day. Was this encounter with a dull metallic flying craft a meeting with purpose? Was this the day that for some unknown reason The X Farmer and his friend were observed and perhaps recorded and maybe even kept track of for years and years?

Were they unknowingly part of an experiment that would last for years?

The Frazier Land is tough land for anyone or anything to move through, with some areas having trees with thorns on them that are over 3 inches long. Also, the land is covered in dense brush and heavily wooded with rocky outcrops, treacherous rock cliffs and valleys filled with rocks such as the creek bed at Panther Rock where the water from the cave flows downward to the Kentucky River. If not for humans clearing land and moving into the area, we would have the perfect habitat for a solitary creature such as Bigfoot. But the fact is people do encroach more and more into all animal habitats and in so doing force the animals to move into other areas. In many cases the areas they are forced to move into do not have the needed food and resources for these animals to maintain their population and soon their life cycle is disrupted and they start to weaken as a species. It has been said many times that animals never forget, and perhaps this is true. Perhaps sightings of Bigfoot occur in places where at one time it was safe to be. Perhaps when a portal opens the animal on the other side does not know that when they enter it they will not be in a place they thought they would be? They end up in a place that has changed and due to confusion and uncertainly they move and are seen. Or maybe these portals are not something that can be used at will. Maybe they just appear as a doorway in another dimension and the creatures that exist in this otherworld are forced to enter or unknowingly just walk through. No one can say for certain what happens or if portals to and from other dimensional existences actually exist. But one thing can be said for certain. Something brings strange creatures and events to The Frazier Land, and all these creatures and events appear and happen very close to Panther Rock.

CHAPTER 4 - THOSE WHO HAVE SEEN

Many people have seen the creature known as Bigfoot or Sasquatch. But many of those people never tell anyone. They do not want to hear the ridicule of others who live in a world with a mindset that is closed. The closed minded people cannot allow themselves to think that this creature exists. They do so for many reasons and due to their mindset, they can only ridicule and make light of those who come forward and tell what they have seen. However, as time has passed and more and more people have come forward to tell of seeing this large hairy, man-like creature, the realization that this creature exists is becoming more and more accepted worldwide. As with most anything that concerns a large amount of people and so far only exists in stories told by others, it takes volumes of these same type of stories to convince people that something is happening and all these people are not just imagining what they are seeing and not making up these stories for attention or any other reason. They are just telling what they saw.

Almost every year we hear of some newly discovered bird, animal, insect or plant here on our planet. And sometimes, depending on the location, we hear of groups of different types of new animal discoveries. Unfortunately, many people never learn about these new discoveries, which doesn't help to enlighten their closed minds to the fact that what we know now, doesn't always remain that way.

Lynn Hutton

I have read every account of a Bigfoot sighting that I could ever get my hands on. I have listened to every recorded interview and watched every TV or movie production that was available to me concerning any aspect of the creature known as Bigfoot. Many of these stories are somewhat believable, some are not believable but every now and then you come across one that is extremely believable, thus is the case of Lynn Hutton. Lynn Hutton has lived in Anderson County his entire life and is a very likeable man. He and his family have lived in the small community of String Town for many years, which is just a short distance to the south of Lawrenceburg. Like many in this rural part of Kentucky, Lynn has been a hunter for most of his life. It was on a scouting trip to check for a place to deer hunt that Lynn and his young son's lives were changed forever. I can sit here and write about what happened to Lynn and his son, but no matter how I write or what I say, it pales in comparison to hearing this story as told by Lynn himself. The complete interview with Lynn can be found on the DVD, *The Wild Man of Kentucky, The Mystery Of Panther Rock.* I would suggest to anyone with an interest in Bigfoot to purchase this DVD and listen to what is considered one of the most credible eyewitness accounts of a Bigfoot sighting that has ever been recorded.

Lynn and his son were walking down a pathway alongside a dense cedar covered field. They were looking for signs of deer and a good place to setup for deer hunting. They were in an area approximately two miles from Panther Rock. As they were walking along suddenly a large, hairy, manlike creature stepped out of the dense cedars and walked directly in front of them. This creature was within 20 feet of both Lynn and his son. The creature as well as Lynn and his son both flinched when they saw each other. Lynn and his son were both frozen in place as their minds tried to understand what they were seeing. This creature was very tall, thick and heavy. It was covered with long matted hair. The creature had stopped and turned its head to look at Lynn and his son and then it did something extremely odd. It stopped and with its eyes locked on Lynn and his son it walked backwards into the cedars from where it came. Lynn and his son were not only startled, they were scared out of their wits. Lynn grabbed his son and headed back and out of where they were as quickly as he could. It was many years before Lynn or his son told their story. But over time Lynn told some friends and this was how the story came to me. Lynn and I had known each other for many years, we had attended school together and when I found his phone number and gave him a call it was good to speak with an old friend. As I spoke with Lynn about his story I could tell from his voice that he was telling me something he unequivocally believed. I could hear not only the sincerity, but the conviction and honesty of someone who had something happen to him that was damn hard to believe, and damn hard to talk about. I could also still hear the fear in Lynn's voice, even after all the years, as he told of the moment this creature walked out in front of him and his son, and changed their lives forever.

The one aspect of this story that I found extremely interesting was how the creature walked backwards with its head turned toward Lynn and his son and reentered the cedar covered land. This aspect of his sighting just made me think about the mind of this creature and what it was thinking at this moment. Its coherent mind and its humanlike response to walking into a situation that not only surprised it but made it realize it could be in danger. The creature did not attack, it did not show aggression, it did not freeze and stand still like it was petrified nor did it run away. It calmly backtracked its way exactly where it had come from, slowly and methodically retreating into the wilderness. The eyewitness states that the creature never lost eye contact with them until they fled. This one moment in this sighting event tells a great deal about this creature we call Bigfoot. From this sighting we find a non-aggressive creature that apparently holds no ill will toward man and has no desire to hurt or interact with man. We have a creature that is intelligent enough to calmly retreat while watching the humans who have startled it, a creature smart enough to not panic and possibly get itself killed or injured. We have a creature that shows many levels of understanding and thought along with a level of intellect that many would think impossible from a creature many consider a savage, unintelligent animal. We see a creature that actually acts like us, in many ways.

The account of this sighting is extremely detailed and hearing his testimony on the DVD is something everyone should take the time to listen to. I think Lynn Hutton will be considered one of the most credible witnesses to ever be documented in the sighting of the illusive and mysterious creature known as Bigfoot.

Bruce Young

Bruce Young and his friend decided it would be a good time to go for a ride and enjoy the late afternoon while riding the back roads of Anderson County. As they rode along they talked about cars, hunting and girls. As they were cruising down Hammond Creek Road Bruce glanced up and as he did he saw something moving along the top of a hill. He stopped the car and told his friend to look up there and see what he was seeing. Bruce jumped out of the car and stood staring at the middle line of the hill and this creature he was watching move along the top. It was just after sunset but there was plenty of light to see this creature. He described it as being seven feet tall or more, huge in size and to him it looked like a massively built, hairy, manlike creature. He stood for what he thought was maybe 30 seconds watching the creature move along. Bruce was approximately 50-60 yards away and he said as he watched he realized he was having what is known as, "goose bumps" appear all over his body. Bruce said the creature moved in what he described as an easy gait, and the hair was long and dark brown. Bruce Young viewed nature much differently after that moment. His thoughts on life and nature were altered. He was a changed man, and what changed his life was a huge, hairy, manlike creature known as Bigfoot.

Philip Spencer

In the early 1970's my friend and I were riding in the Glensboro area of Anderson County. Glensboro is a small town in the western part of Anderson County that sits on the Salt River. It is a beautiful little town which is divided by U.S. 44. As you drive through Glensboro you enter a straight section of road then the road takes several turns as it meanders through the rich, river bottom, farm land. Before you start up a long hill you come to a point where a gravel road turns to the left and if you drive up this road you will eventually arrive at a gate that marks the last part of the road that can be accessed by public vehicles. The land beyond this point is protected by the government because it is a wildlife habitat and is the valley where the Salt River flows and feeds Taylorsville Lake. This area is breathtaking, with sections of the shallow river flowing and cutting its way through the soil and leaving water cut sculptures along the river banks. Remote and not over populated by man, this area holds a rich and diverse group of animals. Late one night my friend and I saw one of the animals that most have never seen and likely never will.

We were riding along at approximately 2 a.m. and as we rode I would hold a powerful spotlight out the passenger window and shine it slowly into and across the valleys and we would look for deer and other animals. It was so much fun to find animals and see their eyes in the night time. We both loved animals and we both liked the night and so this was something we enjoyed doing and we did it on many occasions. But this night would be different. As we approached the last curve before the big hill I shone the light into the last field on the left. This field was the entrance point to where the river turned to the left and then flowed several miles to the Taylorsville Lake. This was also the last area with a few open fields before the land turned to heavy brush and thick trees. As I shone the light through the field we saw many deer so we were talking about how many there were and how their eyes glowed when I would hit them with the light. As I swept the bottom land I was moving the light to the left and as I did I stopped because I thought I saw something strange. I asked my friend if he saw it. He said no and asked what I was talking about. I told him to come to a complete stop and back up a slight bit and get us to where the trees on the left side of the road were not blocking our view at all. He did and then stopped. I took the light and placed it back on top of the passenger side of the car and started sweeping the field again in the area where something kind of out of place had caught my eye. As I swept the area I saw it again, this time I stopped the light on this creature and it was then that we could see the eyes clearly in the light. This creature was huge and it eyes were huge compared to the deer eyes. We had numerous deer in view and this gave us something to judge size with. We both knew this area well and how the land laid so we had a good perspective of what we were seeing collectively. This creature was at least 7 feet tall or taller. We watched as it looked at the light and we could see the eyes. The eyes seemed a reddish orange and as we spoke to each other about what this was the creature turned and started moving away. We could not see it as if it were daylight, however even at this distance, we could easily tell that it was walking upright on two legs. The creature moved steadily down the valley and through the field. I kept the light on it and we watched as it walked in a lumbering, steady stride away from us. Once or twice it looked back over its right shoulder in the direction of where we were sitting. It would then turn its head back around and keep striding along. It came to a fence and it simply walked over it. This was an old barbwire fence and was not in good shape, however it was functional and was still attached to the fence posts that held it in place. The creature never broke stride as it crossed the fence it just walked directly over it and disappeared into the night. We both sat and looked at each other and after a few seconds we just smiled and drove off. We never talked much about this incident but when we did we spoke of how we know for sure at least one exists, as we both saw the large, hairy, upright creature known as Bigfoot.

It was years later when I was walking down the gravel road that runs along the bottom land fields of Salt River that I had another encounter with something. I had parked my truck at the gate and had just started walking back into the area to go to a place where the river widened and deepened which was where I would fish. Just a short distance down the old gravel road the hillside to the right becomes extremely steep and rather tall. As I entered this area I heard a loud sound and suddenly in front of me a very large deer burst out from the hillside, shot across the road into the dense brush and then tore across the fields as fast as it could go. I would get a glimpse of it every now and then as it jumped and ran. Something had really spooked it. As I stood in the road I heard a sound up on the hillside. It was like something big was moving. At first I thought it must be another deer, maybe a buck? But it was then I realized that whatever was up on that hillside was not a deer. I could hear it walking in the woods. This hillside is densely covered with brush and trees, basically impossible to see through, and would be extremely hard to walk through. The hillside was also very steep yet I could hear something moving along somewhat steadily. I could hear whatever this was breaking large limbs. It was hard to tell if the limbs were being broken off old trees or torn off healthy trees, but I certainly could hear limbs snapping from time to time as whatever this was moved along. At times I could also hear sounds made by something large walking, I could hear footsteps but they had a sound to them that made me think whatever this was must be carrying lots of weight. I stood motionless other than when I slowly eased my Buck knife out of its sheath and then held it in my right hand. I listened as whatever this was moved across the hillside and then started down the far side. I knew that on the far side was a small clearing and in it was an old barn or some kind of old building. I moved slowly but steadily. I tried to move when the creature moved and stop when it stopped. I moved quicker as I was sure whatever this was would come off the hillside and move into the open area where the old building was. I was just not fast enough to get to the area in time to see what came off the hillside. I could hear it moving down the hillside toward the clearing and then no sounds as it apparently moved into the clearing. When I reached the area of the old building I looked around very carefully but I saw and heard nothing. Behind the old building was a ravine and it seems I remember a creek bed so whatever this was could have easily moved up the ravine and creek bed out of sight. I walked around this small cleared area and even walked back behind the building, but I saw nothing.

As I walked over to the area of the hillside where the creature would have come down I saw nothing until I looked up on the hillside about 6 to 8 feet. The ground was disturbed and a limb had been moved in a scraping way. The limb was pushed down the hillside a few feet as if something had stepped on it and pushed it down. I walked up to the limb and looked at the disturbed dirt above it. The dirt looked freshly disturbed to me and I believed whatever this was had come off this hillside right where I was standing and as it did it stepped on this limb and pushed the limb down the hill. As I walked back out of the small clearing I looked across the fields where the deer had run and realized that I could see that old fence, still up but in bad shape, where we had watched the Bigfoot walk across the fence late that night. I walked on down the old gravel road and reached my fishing hole and went about my fishing. But the entire time I was there my mind was not really on the fish. I was thinking about what might be out there, what might be watching me, and in my mind, it was Bigfoot.

CHAPTER 5 - RED EYES, THE CEDAR BROOK HOWDY

Every small town has its stories and tall tales. They are told around kitchen tables and campfires and handed down through families over the years. A long running story in Anderson County is the story of the Cedar Brook Howdy or Red Eyes. Cedar Brook is located in the eastern part of Anderson County not far from the small town of Tyrone. The little road that turns to gravel takes you back into a beautiful area that dead ends. It is back in this area that the tales of this monster spring from. The story goes that an unfriendly creature with glowing red eyes lives back in that area. I had heard this story many times over the years but to get a current view on this creature we decided to contact Anderson County resident, paranormal investigator and expert, Jeff Waldridge.

Jeff is not only a paranormal investigator but is well known in the investigative and research community nationwide. I called Jeff and arranged an interview with the Reality Investigative Team so we could gather all the current information he had on the Cedar Brook Howdy. As with everyone else, Jeff was not sure exactly how the creature got its name but he did have a chilling story of how this creature got to be known as an unfriendly beast. The story goes that a young boy and girl were parking under the railroad bridge back in Cedar Brook. They heard something outside and when they looked up they saw these two large, red eyes peering into the passenger side window. The girl screamed and the boy started the car and took off as fast as he could. Just as they were pulling away they heard a strange sound like something scraping the door, only it was deep and loud. They drove back to Lawrenceburg so the boy could take the girl home. As he was walking back to his car after walking her to her door, he noticed that something looked unusual about his passenger side front door. As he approached the car his eyes grew wide and his heart pounded. On the top of the door just below the window bottom were three long, deep gouges. They looked to have been made by huge claws. Many other stories are told in Anderson County and Lawrenceburg by numerous individuals about what they have seen in the Cedar Brook area. Some say it is a mutation, an animal that unfortunately stumbled into the area of Cedar Brook where years ago there was an environmental disaster and due to this the animal became a mutated species. Some say it is a demon like creature, some have even said it is the devil. Almost all the stories have one thing in common and that is the red eyes. So what do we have at Cedar Brook in Anderson County? Is this all just over active teenage imagination fueled by youth and a story told so many times it takes on a life of its own and then becomes a fact? What many do not know is that the story is not complete. A very important part is missing.

Cedar Brook and the small town of Tyrone are also within The Frazier Land, as a matter of fact, they are both just a few miles from the cave known as Panther Rock. The valleys and creeks that lay in the bottoms of the steep cliff sides along the Kentucky River hold many stories. In this area something has been haunting the night for years. The old ones know of it and I know of it. Tyrone and Cedar Brook are only separated by hills and creeks and maybe a mile lies between the two. The creeks of Cedar Brook and Tyrone connect back in the bottoms and they all flow downward to the river. I worked at a stone quarry near the town of Tyrone. The quarry sat beside the Kentucky River and was located under the Tyrone Bridge. I worked as security from 6 at night till 6 in the morning. I worked alone but had numerous friends in Tyrone as well as in Lawrenceburg and Anderson County and to help the night pass we all talked on our CB radios. One night at approximately 4 a.m. I was sitting in my truck in the middle of an open area in the quarry. To my left was a valley known as Six Creeks and to my right was the Kentucky River. It was a nice night and I had my window down and I had my dog with me, his name was Bandit and he was an English Setter. Bandit was laying in the passenger seat sound asleep. I was just sitting looking out the front window at the night sky to the west above the Wild Turkey Distillery. Suddenly in a field to my left which was the first field into the area of Six Creeks, came a scream. It was more like a scream/roar. It is very hard to even describe the volume of this sound. Bandit shot straight up and hit his head on the ceiling of the cab and as he did I fell to my right and grabbed my pistol. I then leaned on Bandit, who was growling and looking out the driver side window, I pointed the pistol toward the window as I was expecting something to attack us through it.

Bandit and I sat frozen in place glancing at each other, not knowing what had just happened. We both stayed focused in the direction of the field across from the quarry and Bandit would growl and then whimper. As we sat there my mind was going a million miles an hour trying to understand what had made a sound so powerful. Then it happened again. This time the sound was further away but still as powerful which made my blood run cold. Bandit moved over me and growled deep in his chest. He was afraid but had moved over me to try and protect me from whatever this was. My heart was pounding so hard it felt like it would push through my chest. I pushed Bandit off me and sat up more, still with my pistol pointing in the direction of the sound. I then realized how quiet it was. There were no sounds at all, just dead silence. But then something happened that made me shake. The town of Tyrone is so close to the quarry that it seems almost part of it, as they are only separated by a small bridge. Tyrone is a small town, just barely big enough to be a town. With perhaps 50 to 70 homes along the river. The Wild Turkey Distillery sits at the top of the hill and then just a short distance from the top of the hill is the Anderson County Humane Society facility. Cedar Brook runs along the west behind this area. This is where the Humane Society shelters homeless animals. As with any small rural town Tyrone and its residents have many dogs.

As we sat and listened to the quiet all at once it started. I had heard this sound before but I had never heard it like I was hearing it now. All the dogs in Tyrone and all the dogs at the Humane Society began moaning. The sound was a mix between a moan and a howl. This sound was slow and drawn out. I had heard the old ones refer to this as a "death howl." The dogs all started at the same time, I could not believe I was hearing this and I could not grasp how they all started at the same time. The sound simply made my soul tremble. With this haunting, moaning howl like sound in the night, coming from above me and below me, I sat and listened for what seemed like five minutes. Bandit sat next to me, almost glued to my side. His ears were perked up but he never made a sound and he never stopped looking out the driver's side window. Just as suddenly as it had started, the dogs all stopped. I rolled my windows up and decided to go inside the office till it was time to go home. Bandit and I sat in the office and it was like we had nothing to say to each other. As if we were two people instead of a man and his dog and something had happened to us and we were not sure what to think or say about what had occurred.

The next day I spoke with Ray Beasley in Tyrone and I told him what had happened, he looked at me and said "so you heard it too." I asked what he meant and he said others had heard the sound also. He said late one night his daddy had not only heard the sound but the morning after he heard the same sound as I described, he found huge, strange, manlike, footprints in the mud of the river bank. His daddy told him the tracks just seemed to come from nowhere and go nowhere but were plain as could be. Is this the same creature that haunts the area of Cedar Brook, is this the Cedar Brook Howdy, Old Red Eyes? The Tyrone and Cedar Brook areas are basically one and the same. The land called Six Creeks actually connects the two areas.

This is not the first time I had heard this sound. In the early 1970's I was riding late one night on Hammonds Creek Road. Hammonds Creek Road is located in the northern section of Anderson County and could be considered northwest. It was a summer night and I had my window down and was just doing what everyone did who lived out in the country; I was riding the back roads killing time. With my arm resting on the door and some music playing on the radio I came to a steep hill and as I was about half way down it something happened. To my left was a ditch and a wire fence. All at once something screamed right beside my car. This scream was like a scream and roar combined. It was so powerful it felt like it had a concussion affect it. I slammed on my brakes out of reflex and realized I was leaning to the right side of my seat. I grabbed my pistol and turned to the window and pointed my gun. In my mind every monster ever known was coming through that window. Any second I was going to be dead. I had almost driven into the ditch on the right side of this narrow road so I knew I needed to get out of this place quickly. I sat up and drove away as fast as I could. My heart was pounding hard as I drove and tried to think about what had just happened to me. This scream/roar was so powerful it made me think that a dinosaur or some kind of bizarre monster had made it. The concussion affect was stunning. I have thought this many times and I am still not sure if it really was a type of concussion from the power of this sound or perhaps it was just due to the intensity and apparent loudness that made me think that there was some kind of force project-ed by whatever made the remarkable vocalization. The sound I heard at Hammonds Creek was so similar to the sound I heard at Tyrone. The sound at Hammonds Creek was much closer, but the sound at Tyrone had the same characteristics and ferocity so I have no doubt that it had been made by the same creature.

What is it about The Frazier Land that makes it so susceptible to these unexplained and strange events? Every type of unusual, paranormal event has at one time or another taken place in this area. Even ghosts roam The Frazier Land, oh yes, they most certainly do. One day I went into work at the rock quarry at 6 p.m. It was a rainy day and the clouds seemed to lay just on top of the trees. I pulled into the quarry office and parked on the scales used to weigh the trucks coming out with loads of rock. I walked into the office as I did every evening and walked over and opened a soda. The office was built with large windows all around the left side of the structure and from inside you could see down into the quarry and also up the road that went to the top of the hill by the distillery and then on to Lawrenceburg. Approximately 100 yards up the road and up the hill was an old rock road on the left. This old road was called Six Creeks. Across from the entrance to Six Creeks was the upper entrance to the quarry which led down to the underground area. I walked over to the window to look out across the quarry and up the hill. No one was on the property but me. As I walked to the window I raised the drink to my lips and as I moved my head back to take a sip my eyes fell on the area of the road where the entrance to Six Creeks was located. I froze in place.

I stood with the drink almost to my mouth. My eyes were locked onto what I was seeing. My mind was racing trying to grasp what my eyes saw. I stood and watched a woman float out of the entrance to Six Creeks. The woman had her head turned so that she was facing up the hill. She had very long, gray hair and she was wearing a green sweater. She slowly floated out into the middle of the main road, up the hill and then without turning or doing anything, she floated back into the entrance to the old rock road to Six Creeks. I just stood in place, unsure of what had just happened. My mind and body finally merged and I lowered my soda and tried to rationally understand what I had just seen. I took a long drink and as I did I realized something. The woman I saw had no legs. She had no lower body. All I saw was from her waist up. As I stood there staring at the same place trying to decide if I was just seeing things or if the rain and low clouds could be playing tricks on my eyes, it happened again. This time I was absolutely focused on what I was witnessing. The woman did the exact same thing. She floated out of the entrance to the Six Creeks road and she floated to the middle of the road that went up the hill and by the distillery. Without turning, she then floated directly back into the entrance to the old rock road and vanished. This time I saw her clearly, so clearly that it was almost like I wished I had not seen her so clearly. Her hair was long to her waist. The sweater she wore had long sleeves and she had what seemed to be a white colored collar under the sweater. She had no legs and she ended at her waist. It was like where her hair ended so did she.

I stood for a moment then I ran out the door, jumped in my truck and drove up the hill as fast as I could go. I pulled into the entrance to the old rock road and slammed my brakes on and jumped out. The old rock road is a single lane road and as you pull in on your right there is a very steep hillside and on your left is a very deep drop-off. With the ground so wet going up the steep hillside was basically impossible and if anyone had fallen off the ledge, they would still be there, and most likely be in bad shape. I have often looked back on this event and wondered what I was looking for. I saw the woman clearly and I saw her not once but twice. I walked up the hill a short ways as walking any further was impossible. I looked all over the area for footprints and found nothing. I looked over the edge of the drop-off and saw nothing below. I then jumped in my truck and drove all the way back into Six Creeks. I crossed all Six Creeks and looked everywhere a car or truck could be parked back in this area. I checked for footprints, I found nothing and not a person anywhere. I drove back to the quarry and went back into the office and sat down. I slowly drank my drink and thought of what I had just seen. It was then that it came to me, like a bolt of lightning. I had seen this woman before, or at least I thought I had.

Many years before on a hot summer afternoon I drove back into Six Creeks with my girlfriend and we got out at the very last field. While she spread a blanket out to do some sunbathing, I turned my truck around so it was facing toward the way out. I was leaning on the front right bumper and was just about to take a drink of beer when my eyes spotted a large tree down near the end of the field where you crossed the creek and started out of the area. As my eyes took in the big tree I saw something. I rose up and looked closely. Although it was 50-75 yards away, I could see clearly and it looked like an older woman was peeking around the tree. She was leaning out and I could see her long gray hair hanging down over her left shoulder and although I could not see it clearly, it looked like she had on something green. I stood up and reached in the truck for my pistol. When I looked back she was gone. I told the girl to grab the blanket and put some clothes on. She kept asking what was wrong and I just told her I thought I saw someone. I did not tell her exactly what I thought I saw. When I got to the tree there was nothing there. I got out and walked around it and looked on the ground. Not a sign of anything or anybody. We drove on out of Six Creeks and until the event at the quarry I had not given much thought to the woman behind the tree, but I had not forgotten it either.

But the ghosts of The Frazier Land were not done, specifically this ghost. The day after I had my sighting of the floating lady, Wilson Wash came to the quarry to visit me at 11 p.m. He was a security guard at the Wild Turkey distillery and also my close friend. Every night after he made his first round he would drive down to the quarry and we would sit out in the open area in the middle of the huge rock piles and talk for awhile. As he pulled up I could tell he had something to tell me. He pulled his truck up beside mine and rolled his window down and we talked a minute about his vacation before I told him what I had seen the day before. He sat and stared at me and then said I was lying because I had heard what happened back on the railroad tracks on the distillery property. I told him I had no idea what he was talking about. He then realized I was serious and he just sat and looked forward out his windshield for a moment then he turned to face me and told me what had happened.

Three or four days before my sighting of the floating woman a maintenance worker at the distillery had walked back down the railroad tracks to check on a piece of machinery that was sitting near them. The distillery sometimes parked or left equipment back in this area as they owned the property along the tracks. It was just about dusk when the man arrived and he had taken his young son with him. As he was working on the engine of the piece of equipment his son suddenly said, "Daddy who is that woman?" The man turned and looked at his son and asked what he was talking about. It was just between daylight and darkness and the boy turned and pointed behind the man and said "that woman." The man turned and he saw a woman floating into the darkness. The woman had long gray hair and she was wearing a green sweater and she seemed to just vanish from her waist down. The man stood and watched as she just floated into the night and was gone. He turned, picked his son up and then walked quickly along the railroad tracks back to his truck. He told my friend the story of what happened two days before I saw the floating lady. I must point out that I had not told anyone what I saw yet. He had no way of knowing what I saw until I told him and later I saw the man who saw the floating lady and he told me the exact same story my friend had told me. In the next few days I saw several residents of Tyrone and asked them about this floating lady and they said they had heard others talk of seeing a woman at night along the road in that area. They said she had long gray hair and would be moving along the road's edge and they never saw her face.

Near the property where the cave is located was an old farm, back on the farm was an old house that a couple friends of mine were renting. My girlfriend and I had gone back to visit them, and then around 1 a.m. we left and were slowly driving up the gravel road. I of course knew about the cave and also had heard lots of strange stories about this part of the county. For many years I had heard the daughter of the property owners talk about a light that would float through the field near a barn a short distance from the gravel road we were driving on. As we slowly turned a corner on the road I saw a light over in the field, this was a clear night, the moon was bright and the land was well illuminated. My girlfriend saw this light also and asked what it was. I stopped the car and we watched the light floating slowly through the field. There was no one with the light, because we would have easily seen them. The light had such a strange look to it, similar to an old lantern which was floating about 8-10 feet off the ground. We watched the light go all the way through the field and then move to the front of the barn. I then drove to the end of the gravel road, turned left and went to the barn. Although my girlfriend was not in favor of my getting out, I did and she rolled up the windows and locked the doors after I did. I walked up to the barn and checked everything around it. I saw nothing and heard nothing, the barn doors were closed.

Something moves through the night in the Cedar Brook area and has done so for many years. So for all of you who simply laugh and write-off the Cedar Brook Howdy as a tale told for amusement, you might want to stop and rethink your ideas. Something lurks in the night in this area and it is not a figment of the imagination. Something lurks in the night in many areas of Anderson County and it just might be a large, hairy, bipedal, creature referred to as Bigfoot …

INTO THE FRAZIER LAND

From the east and west coasts and Europe, they journeyed to Kentucky - an eclectic group of individuals with a purpose. Philip Spencer, Kat Drake, O.H. Krill, Philip Gardiner, Matt Clark and Tony Gerard. These people make up the Reality Entertainment Investigative Team. Collectively they have a huge number of years in researching events and stories about everything and anything within the world of the paranormal. But one specific part of this wild and mysterious subject matter that they all have in common is a deep set interest in the creature known as Bigfoot. Philip Spencer and Philip Gardiner had been close friends for many years and O.H. Krill met Philip Gardiner as they are both published by Reality Press. Matt Clark who is the guitarist for the band FreakHouse also met Philip Gardiner as his band is on Reality Entertainment (the company's music division). Tony Gerard has been intrigued with the illusive creature known as Bigfoot since he was a child and his quest continues to find out the truth concerning this creature. When I told Philip Gardiner about all the strange events occurring in Kentucky he became extremely interested and we started exchanging information about this case. The one specific that caught Gardiner's eye was the first unexplained animal track. To this day no one is sure what made this track but Gardiner and I both know enough to know this was a very odd track and whatever made it was a large animal. As time went on, the four of us exchanged emails and as more and more information came in concerning the strange events from the past as well as the present, we all knew it was time to head for Kentucky and investigate the area and the cave. In April of 2008 the team converged on the bluegrass state and an investigation began that none of us would ever forget and for some it would be a life changing event.

Having been gone from my hometown for many years it was good to be back and see all the places and people who had been such an important part of my life. The team gathered at a local hotel and after sitting and discussing all we had to do, we loaded our equipment and rolled out into the beauty of Anderson County and the town of Lawrenceburg. One of our first stops was to the Anderson Public Library where we met with the director, Jeff Sauer. Mr. Sauer was very helpful and allowed us to sit in the historical research section and look over one of the rare copies of *Panther Rock*. As we sat and looked through the book it gave us a feeling of being in the area during that time period and we all felt we were reading a true document which portrayed the area as it was at the time of the writing. As the words are read one can see how hard times were and how people then were very helpful to others but also very conscious of their safety. They were well aware of how the land and people outside of their immediate families could do things that might quickly end their lives. But it was the mysterious side of the story in the book that lured us to the library and to the book itself. We noticed that although the book was published in 1931 the story referenced strange tales of the cave known as Panther Rock which seemed to date back to the mid-late 1700's. Within the book was the story of the large panther that killed a Native American chief on the ledge above the Panther Rock cave. This part of the book was of great interest to us as we had heard numerous stories of large black cats in the area as well as stories of Bigfoot and other strange and unexplainable animals and their tracks or damage.

After our visit to the library we headed west in Anderson County to the little town of Glensboro and to a place that would always be part of the reason I was and am so interested in the paranormal and especially Bigfoot. We drove to the location where I had seen the creature late one night as it moved through a river bottom and out of sight. It was a rather odd feeling standing and looking out across the river bottom and feeling all the feelings one gets when they encounter something like this creature, all over again. As I stood there I felt as if something that was part of me was out in this land and it was somewhere out of sight, yet I felt like it was aware of the fact I was there. As my eyes focused on the area where I saw the creature moving away into the night so many years ago, I could see the lumbering gait, and the way the creature looked back over its right shoulder as it walked away. A connection seemed to have taken place when the creature looked back over its shoulder in the direction of the vehicle we were in. I have heard others speak of feeling a bonding or connection after an encounter with the legendary creature and I for one believe there is a reason for this. Maybe in some abstract way we are seeing ourselves as we used to be or perhaps we are seeing ourselves as we should be, creatures at peace with the earth and all its inhabitants and wonders.

Over the few days we traveled the roads of Anderson County meeting with numerous witnesses and listening as they told their stories about strange creatures, sounds and events. One day we drove to the Gilberts Creek area which is just a few miles from Panther Rock and considered part of The Frazier Land. The primitive look of this area near the Kentucky River takes one's mind and wraps it in a world that has been gone for ages. Once you are within the rock walls and creek covered valleys and you see the dense wooded hillsides you can easily understand how animals of any type would find this area perfect to exist and flourish in while not being seen. We stopped along the road where the two men saw the animal walk across on its hind legs. A wolf like creature, only much larger with a protruding stomach, that looked straight forward and vanished into the woods. An event in their lives that changed them forever. We drove to an area where two concrete slabs are used as bridges and we stood as I pointed to them and told the story of my friend and his encounter with a huge black cat on the hillside. How many other stories are known that are never told publicly about what goes on in The Frazier Land? What is it that makes this part of the earth so conducive to having things of this nature occur?

In the afternoon we drove to the farm of Ann and Darrel Gabhart who own the land where Panther Rock is located. Darrel and Ann are like all the people of Anderson County in that they greeted us with a smile and offered to help us in any way they could. Darrel even drove some of us in his truck to an area close to the cave as Ann and the others walked through the rolling hills to the cave. In the daytime the cave and the area is without a doubt breathtakingly beautiful. Thick woods and lush foliage abound. Darrel, who has a great knowledge of the area, told us the story of the Native American chief being killed by a large cat on the ledge above the cave. While Ann, a well known author and lover of nature, took others down to the cave to get a closer look. We saw the tree where the strange clippings were found and Darrel pointed out to us that one side appeared dead. He said the tree had been in good condition before the strange clippings were found but now it seems to be dying. Our daytime trip to Panther Rock was informative and peaceful, but we had plans to return in a few days, only this time at night.

After our visit with Ann and Darrel we drove to The X Farmer's residence and settled in for a long interview with him. So many unusual events have taken place on The X Farmer's land we decided to go into the heart of it for our interview. We hiked into the area where the rock cairns are located and which is also the area where the mysterious sound has been heard many times. We also were in the area where the strange animal track with the canine and feline characteristics was found. We set up our equipment and while being surrounded by strange rock structures within The Frazier Land, I interviewed The X Farmer. The sincerity and honesty of his account of the events made for gripping listening. None of us doubted anything he told us as he told it just like he had always said it had happened, no matter which events he was talking about. At times you could hear in his voice how when the events were happening he was not sure what to do, he was uncertain of the reality of what he was hearing and seeing. After interviewing The X Farmer we packed up our gear and hiked up and out of the area and moved on to the next stop. We had arranged to return to The X Farmer's land the next night which would be a night we would never forget.

On our way out of the area where The X Farmer lived we stopped and talked to the couple who owned the cow that was attacked. Once again we met good people who took the time to stop their work and talk with us about what happened. This was the first time I had heard this story directly from the cow's owners who witnessed the events. I was very surprised to learn that the cow's right eye was also torn out and that the cow had made its way from a back field all the way to the couple's house and crashed through a gate. I also learned the cow had a young calf that it most likely was trying to protect. The possibility of dogs doing this was discussed but the husband stated that he didn't think that was the case. He is a man who has spent his life farming, hunting and enjoying the outdoor. He is someone who knows the land and the animals and what goes on in the woods and in the land he owns. He said he was not sure what did this to his cow, but he felt it was not dogs. He was inclined to believe that it was possibly a very large cat or even some other kind of animal, as to what, he could not say.

Over the years I have read, listened to and watched many interviews with individuals who have had strange occurrences happen to them. I have also interviewed and spoken with numerous individuals who have had strange events happen to them. I must say that Lynn Hutton is without a doubt one of the most believable and sincere people I have ever interviewed. His story is straight forward and told with an intensity that I believe comes from someone who has had something very unusual happen to them. As I have written before, writing about what Lynn Hutton and his son saw is nothing compared to watching and hearing it from Lynn. When you watch the DVD and hear his story you will see the sincerity and feel the compelling passion he has in him about what he saw that day. What the creature did when it walked out in front of Lynn and his son still makes me stop and ponder. To me it tells many things about the creature's mind. It stops, it looks directly at Lynn and his son, it then simply moves back into the cedars and vanishes. However it is the way it went back into the woods that sticks in my mind. It moved backwards, and it moved backwards with its eyes locked on Lynn and his son and never turned its head back or hesitated. From listening to Lynn's description of this event several times, it is as if the creature went into reverse slow motion. Simply retracing its exact steps back into where it came from. It did not attack, it did not scream, it did not freeze, it did not run away, it did not move toward Lynn or his son. Of all the things we would think it might do, it did none of them. A huge, long haired, manlike creature that walks out of a cedar thicket directly in front of a man and his son and when it realizes what it has done it just stops, looks at them, retains eye contact and then moves backwards into the place it came out of.

Coherent thought, rational thinking, logical reaction, compassionate understanding, responding and not reacting, awareness of a situation that could have been violent yet not doing anything to make the violent reaction occur. All these aspects and more make up some part of what this creature did. A little of each is in this creature's response to this event. So what if a little of each of the components can be found in the creature's response? Each of these components require intelligence, they require a thought process that I consider above a primal animalistic re-action. The response was not induced by the primal rush of adrenaline that we get when we are in danger, the situation was analyzed and an intelligent response was implemented. Listen and watch Lynn Hutton tell his story, and as you do you will feel what he felt. You will be part of that moment in which his and his son's lives were changed forever.

I am now going to invert events and tell of our visit to Panther Rock at night before I write of our night on The X Farmer's land. Tony Gerard arrived and joined our group so we loaded our gear and headed out for a night at Panther Rock. We arrived just before dark and Tony, O.H. and Philip Gardiner went down to the cave for a closer inspection. Matt and I remained on top of the cave and we positioned ourselves on a rock ledge that comes out of an open area above it. As night arrived I sat and thought back on all the days and nights I had spent at this place. All the good times my friends and I had. I thought of the history and the stories about Panther Rock. As I sat in the darkness and listened to the woods my mind drifted back to the night when I was awakened by someone hitting me on the back and screaming, "Look, Look, Look!" And when I rolled over I saw a bluish, white light coming from the cave, a light that did not look like any light one would see anywhere. The light had a quality to it that was so different it is hard to describe. I thought of the three men who were in the cave and lowered their friend into one of the holes in the floor until he screamed and then explained later that he saw the devil.

Tony, Philip and O.H. came back up from the cave and decided to move around in the woods and listen for any sounds they could hear. Matt and I remained in the area above the cave to do the same. There is a feeling that could be described as "ancient" about Panther Rock. Of course Panther Rock is ancient but when you enter the area you get a feeling of being somewhere else, as if you have actually stepped back in time and something is about to occur. I have always had that feeling about Panther Rock. Perhaps the shadow I saw that moved against the woods is something that is ancient and is at Panther Rock to protect it? Maybe it is a guardian or gatekeeper? Something that must be there to guide whatever comes through a dimensional portal into this dimension? Or does this shadow creature hold the key to the door? Questions without answers, but questions that will be asked over and over by those who spend time in areas like Panther Rock. Overall the night at Panther Rock was uneventful, we heard some sounds and once we even thought we heard some distant knocks, but over all a quiet night, but after the night before on The X Farmer's property, we deserved a quiet night, the night before was filled with events that will be with us all forever.

Now I will tell of the night before our trip to Panther Rock. We decided to spend a night in the back of The X Farmer's property before we went to Panther Rock. We made this decision as we expected the night visit to Panther Rock to be a night filled with events and sounds. We were wrong, it was the trip to The X Farmer's land that would be the night that we are all still trying to understand and figure out just exactly what happened. Tony had not arrived yet so it was Philip Gardiner, O.H. Krill, Matt Clark and I who made the trip to The X Farmer's property. We used a 4 wheel drive vehicle and a tractor to get us to the area we wanted to set up our gear in and make our central campsite. We arrived just a little before dusk and we spent the time until dark getting all our cameras and devices ready. As darkness took the land O.H. and Philip G. decided to venture down a steep path into the area of the cairns - the same area where The X Farmer had heard The Frazier Sound. Matt and I stayed at the campsite and monitored the area with night vision. We used two way radios to stay in touch and about five minutes after O.H. and Philip G. went into the woods we heard the radio chirp and heard O.H. say, "Something is happening, something is watching us. Whatever it is, it is moving in the trees, we can hear it." Matt and I responded and then we started listening to the night. Suddenly we heard something to our left then to our right. It was the same sound but it was like it was on our left then quickly moved to our right. We could hear the trees move as if something was moving through them rapidly. It made no sense as to how this was happening. We stood and listened and as we did we could hear something moving in the tree line. We were in a large open field and near the north tree line. The air felt odd, like it was intense. We stood and listened and watched. We both felt like we were being watched and like something was just inside the tree line. At that moment O.H. and Philip G. came back up the path. The four of us sat and talked about what was happening in this place. Philip G. stated something was following them, they could hear it moving through the trees. O.H. described how the sound made him think that something was flying or floating through the dense woods. Matt and I agreed that what we heard was the same. Like something was in the trees and was moving through them as if they were not solid.

As we sat, Philip G. looked to the east, slowly stood up, pointed and whispered softly "look." We all turned and looked and we could see a light. It was just floating near a group of trees and brush in the middle of the field. Philip G. took off running toward the light. We all stood and moved in the same direction. As we were moving we noticed another light in the woods. It was a bluish, white light and we could see it in the distance through the trees. As I was looking at the light in the woods I saw something I will never forget. I saw something move between myself and the light. It was hard to tell what it was or how far away it was, the distance between us and the light in the woods was very hard to calculate or gauge. But whatever I saw made a distinct shadow as it moved in the air between my location and the light in the woods. It was about this time that Philip G had an experience he will never forget. As he was walking near the tree line he saw a shadow float out of the woods and go back in. He said he saw this clearly and was certain of what he saw, because this was the very first event of this type he had ever seen. Here we were in the area where the old rock cairns, the rock fence and the sound called home. We were all part of something, what it was we didn't know. We each were affected by this night and this place. Something was there, something was watching us, and something was (in my opinion) engaging us on a mental level. It seemed as if whatever it was, was almost playing with us, testing us, messing with our minds as they say. We heard distinct knocks in the woods. We heard the limbs and leaves in the trees moving and we heard them rustle as if something was flowing through them like water. There was fluidity to the sound and the movement. The "ancient" feeling had encompassed all of us. At the time I felt as if we were in a place where time had stopped, as if we were on The X Farmer's land but somehow we were not. Just down the hill was the place where The X Farmer found the strange canine/feline track. A short distance away was the place where The X Farmer found the 18 plus inch footprint. We were surrounded by all these events and surrounded was how we felt. We found ourselves looking around constantly, as if we must stay on guard. Sounds would come from one side, then the exact same sound, just seconds later would come from the other side of where we were. It was as if our entire environment had morphed into a surreal dreamlike state. What was happening to us and what was doing this to us? We felt displaced, we felt out of time as if we were not exactly in the moment.

As we were caught in this vortex of strangeness I realized something. This is how Panther Rock used to feel. This is how the area around the cave and the woods around the cave felt, the air was electric at times and lights and sounds were common. So had whatever manifested itself at Panther Rock moved? Was it now residing on The X Farmer's land or was it just simply luring us into a false sense of tranquility by an uneventful night before at Panther Rock. Perhaps we were getting too close? Perhaps something needed protecting or guarding? The area where the rock cairns are located is surrounded by a rock wall. Within this area, which consists of over 12 acres, are many strange rock formations. Not all are the cairns in the pictures in the DVD. Slab like structures have been found as well as other rock formations that are definitely manmade, but no one is sure what exactly the purpose of these rock structures could be. The area that the old rock fence surrounds is not land that anyone would consider good land to build on. The land is on a slope. Instead of finding a nice level or semi-level piece of land to build on, whoever did this chose a sloped hillside that grows steeper as you near the bottom of the area. Many reasons could be conjured up as to why build on this piece of land and then put a rock fence around it. However it is rather odd that of all the land around, this was the area chosen. Maybe it was a gift to someone or it was just the land that was available. Or perhaps it was chosen because something very special was here. Maybe something very secret was on the land? No foundation has been found within the surrounding area. Much of the area is basically impassible as the brush and woods are so thick with vines and thickets it would take forever to cut through. Was this area any different hundreds of years ago? It would seem the answer would be no as all the old timers say it's been like that for as far back as anyone knows.

So upon a steep hillside something was encompassed by a rock fence. As to what is on or in the property no one can say for sure. As we looked back and discussed what had happened to us on that night on The X Farmer's property we realized how we were manipulated, how we were drawn away from the fenced in area. Philip G. and O.H. had walked into the darkness and taken the trail to the north of the fenced in area. They heard something come from the area of the rock fence and it moved across the spot they were in and to the east. Once this happened their attention was not in the direction of the cairns, it was to the east of that area. Matt and I were stationed at the top of the section in an open field. We first heard something in the area of the rock fence and cairns only it sounded like it was to the south slightly. What we heard was a loud sound like a limb being broken. Then we heard sounds like something moving in the trees only not on the ground. Then almost instantly we heard the same sounds to our right which was to the east and our attention was immediately moved to this area and once we thought about this later, I realized we had been lured away from the area of the fence and cairns. We were not only lured away but we were made to focus on the exact opposite location of the cairns and rock fence. Our attention was now to the east where Panther Rock was approximately 1500 yards away. How interesting that we were being lured in the direction of the cave as if an invisible force was steering us in that direction. Lights appeared from nowhere and danced in the field. Shadows came alive and moved in the night. Sounds beckoned from the tree line as if to call us. And all of them pointed east, not back west to the cairns and fenced in area, but to the east. It was almost funny to realize how obvious the manipulation was. Not only did it work, it worked perfectly. We kept walking and running to the east trying to get near to the lights or trying to see them clearer and as we did, the lights would appear further to the east. Drawing us away, and taking us from the place where we had started. The place we had visited, walked and looked at. The place where strange and bizarre events occur so often they almost seemed common place, or like The X Farmer said, "It's just something that we are used to." I have always felt that somewhere in the area of Panther Rock a portal might exist, a door to another dimension, and if so, why not another or perhaps something came through a portal and took up residence on The X Farmer's land. Or maybe in this place older than time itself something sleeps, and while it sleeps it is guarded because it must not be disturbed.

As the night crept on we all became exhausted. As if our minds had been drained and our ability to think rationally was taken. We all stood looking in all directions around us, as if we were looking and waiting for something to come again, to once more attack us in spirit and soul. We finally gathered ourselves and loaded up our gear and slowly made our way back to The X Farmer's home and then into my van and off into the night we drove. Little was said on the way back, our minds, bodies and souls had taken a hearty beating in the field. Later we also realized that we seemed to have lost our grasp of time in that field. Had we been edged and slowly moved into place? Into a vortex? Some sort of dimensional portal where we were displaced from our normal existence and thrown off frequency from our standard resonance? Something happened to us in that field, something used us and manipulated us as if we were children and led us away from something it did not want us near. But what did it have to fear from us? What threat did we pose that made it want us out of the area? Was it the fact we were just there and we were looking for it? Was it that we came to find it or was it luring us away from its treasure? Then again maybe the hunter did not like being hunted, maybe it did not like the fact that we walked into its world in the darkness and then walked directly into its house without asking permission to come in? So many questions without answers.

Philip Gardiner had an experience in this field that was a first for him. He saw a shadow move out of the tree line near the ground and then slowly go back into the brush. He said he saw it clearly even in the night. He had absolutely no qualms about what he saw. So once again this shadow creature makes an appearance, just like it did for me many years ago at Panther Rock. Philip G. had no idea what this shadow was and he said so. But as I stood and looked into my friend's eyes as he told me what he had seen, I could see how much of an impact this event had on him. Philip G. is a super intelligent person who is at heart a skeptic. But for the first time since I have known him, I saw in his eyes and his expression that his brilliant mind was somewhat unsure of its rational and logical processes. He had seen something that did not compute. Something that wasn't supposed to be there had manifested itself to him. I could see his mind churning through his eyes, he was using his genius to grasp what he saw and conclude exactly what it was but he could not. Just as I could not grasp what I saw when the shadow creature moved along the tree line at Panther Rock. Was this exactly what we were supposed to think? Is this what the creature does? Was it chance that both of us saw it? Somewhere in all these questions is an answer that would very likely explain many unknowns, but for now, the unknowns will remain as such.

On July 10, 2008 I received a phone call from The X Farmer. He told me he thought I should call his nephew and hear what he had to say. The X Farmer said his nephew had some information concerning multiple sightings of Bigfoot. I called his nephew and had one of the most interesting conversations I have had with anyone in some time. The nephew told me how he had mentioned the situation on his uncle's farm and all the strange events that occur there to a friend of his from another county and specifically the recorded sound and the huge foot prints found. The nephew's friend then told him that his wife had seen a creature just like what everyone describes as Bigfoot. He said they live in a rural area and she was coming home in the dark. As she turned a curve she saw something on the side of the road near a fence. At first she wasn't sure what it was so she stopped and backed up so her lights would shine on the fence where she had seen it. When her lights hit the fence she saw something that chilled her soul. Straddling the fence was a large, 7 to 8 foot tall creature. It had its hand on the fence and was pushing down on the top as it moved over it. When she had stopped and backed up quickly to shine her lights on the fence it must have made the creature freeze in place. She stated it was a hairy, manlike, creature only so much bigger than any man. She rushed home to tell her husband what had happened. Her husband laughed and told her she was just seeing things and not to be upset about what she thought she saw. Over the next week her husband would see his neighbors or friends around town and he would tell them what his wife said she saw. To his surprise he was not greeted with laughter but he was told over and over that they had also seen the same creature. This all happened outside of Anderson County but is a perfect example of what seems to be an endless string of Bigfoot sightings in the central Kentucky area.

As the nephew and I continued talking, our discussion moved to The X Farmer's land. The nephew had hunted on The X Farmer's land for over twenty years and no one had ever asked him if he had ever had any strange sightings or events happen to him. He began talking to me and telling me about event after event. I could tell there was relief in his voice as he had kept this information to himself but was now ready to tell me what had happened. He knew of the stories of his uncle's land but was not sure on all the specifics. As I listened it was very strange to hear what he had to say. He spoke of the area near the cairns and the rock fence, the area where the sound is often heard and he told how in this area and the creek below he gets a very creepy feeling. The nephew is an extremely well versed outdoorsman who spends a great deal of time in the woods and is familiar with the sights, sounds and the natural state of the woods and forests of Kentucky. He told me of how he was sitting in a deer stand very early one morning and he heard something coming through the woods. However it was not moving like anything he had heard before. He stated it was moving quickly, yet at times he heard what he thought were some kind of muffled footsteps. But he said whatever this was, it was not moving on the ground. It was moving through the trees, and it was moving in a way that confused him, he said it came toward him and then past him and was gone.

He told me of a morning before sunrise when he was down near the same area and watched a light move slowly down a hillside. He said at first he thought it was another hunter moving down the hillside in the dark but soon he realized it was not. It was a white light but somewhat off white. As he stood and watched he noticed the light was floating. He knew this land well, he had been in the exact area where the light was and he knew this was not a person coming down that steep hillside. He watched as the light would float along and move down and at times it would parallel the hillside. It moved slowly and then just as slowly as it had appeared, it was gone.

He told me of the time he took his wife with him back on The X Farmer's land to walk around in the woods and as they entered the creek area near the cairns she stopped and looked at him and said, "This place has a cold feeling to it, like something or someone has died here or is still here." He also told of how very early one morning as he was walking into the cairn area he suddenly felt as if he were being watched. He said he was just suddenly overwhelmed by the feeling. He said he kept walking and even got in his tree stand but the feeling was so overwhelming he finally just descended from the stand and left. As I sat and listened to him it was interesting to hear him talk of all this as much of what he said was exactly or really close to what had happened to all of us in the field that night.

The one thing he spoke of over and over was a feeling. He stated he had the feeling of being watched, the feeling that something was just out of sight and it was following him. His wife spoke of a feeling. She spoke of a feeling as if something very bad happened down in the creek bed near the cairns area. The X Farmer spoke time and time again about how he would feel something, as if something was around him in the air. His family also said they could sense something was out there somewhere in the darkness. The X Nephew spoke of the sounds in the woods and how they were not sounds that someone with over 20 years of outdoor and hunting experience could recognize. How whatever it was would move through the trees, invisible yet making noise. He told of a loud sound he heard, like a deep sounding thump as something heavy walked over a log and somehow raised it and dropped it. This is the exact sound that we heard that night on The X Farmer's land.

In our remaining days in Anderson County we spoke with more people and heard more stories. We were told of the Cedar Brook Howdy A.K.A. Red Eyes by Jeff Waldridge and the horrifying story of how this creature left huge claw marks in a car door. Philip G., Matt, O.H., Tony and I sat in my van beside an old abandoned distillery and listened intently to my cell phone speaker as Bruce Young told us of his sighting of a large, hairy, manlike, creature he saw walking along a ridge line late one afternoon. Time after time we heard tales of people seeing this elusive creature in the woods of Anderson County and not only Bigfoot, but numerous other strange animal sightings and events. We had several large black cat sighting reports, ghosts, lights, sounds, sightings of anomalies in the sky, the list goes on and on. But what stood out were the stories of the creature who is the Wildman of the woods, the Old Man of the Mountains, Sasquatch, or Bigfoot.

Conclusion

Historically the reports of Bigfoot go back as far as records exist. The name or format of description may vary, but the stories remain basically the same. When one starts digging into the factual aspects of terminology and translation of terms and stories specific to Native American lore and beliefs the actual definitions and true meanings of words and stories can be very hard to validate. As with any translation of a complex and often times modified version of a modified version of communication, the interpretation of definition can be used to suit the person needing facts for correlation or verification of a point they are trying to make. When researching all the tales and folklore associated with Bigfoot your mind can soon become numbed by the vast amount of information. Every race and creed of person on this planet has their tales of something that lurks either in the woods or somewhere else with the intent to make us pay for something we have done. It is the classic "Boogyman" syndrome, and with this the stories become confabulated with information that actually has nothing to do with the factual content. And so great tall tales are born and built upon and carried over for years and years. So be the case with the stories of Bigfoot. In the Native American dialects researchers have found numerous words they equate to describing what many call Bigfoot, however upon closer examination these words and stories may not be as specific to the creature as some would like them to be.

When we get into translations and determining what a story means that is written in parables we soon find the translation and interpretation most often suits the person doing the translation or meaning of the story. And the vagueness and internal usage of specific wording by groups in remote locations can totally be misinterpreted to mean what is commonly thought to be a correct definition, yet over time an isolated group can take the term or story and have a totally different meaning than what the common understanding is thought to be.

I have found myself drawing away from the technical definition games and instead seeking out the stories people have to tell about their encounters. I am not saying that good solid research into anything is not important, it most certainly is. It is just that the sheer volume of information and different points of view on interpretation and meaning of modern day and ancient writings eventually numbs my mind and I find myself disengaged from the basic task, of trying to understand what I saw that night in the river bottom near Glensboro in Anderson County, Kentucky.

The psychological aspects to the human need for something to be waiting for us if we do bad, or something to be watching over us so we don't do anything bad is a strange trait we have. Are we such ignorant and uncontrolled creatures that it takes something like a story of a creature lurking in the darkness to make us have conscious and rational concepts and morals? All through history documentation shows the human race has used fables, stories and tales to influence our way of being. But this documentation also shows how when we come face to face with something we cannot understand, we have a tendency to make whatever has brought our thought processes to a halt evil or dark, turning it into something that we must fear. Is this inherent survival instinct fueled by adrenalin? When our minds encounter something that we cannot understand do our primal instincts kick in and our minds stamp whatever it is with the word "danger?" From that point our creative abilities kick in and we then have a dark story that will be passed along through generations and built upon so we can warn others that whatever scared us is evil and bad and we must live in fear of it, even if it doesn't really exist in the way we think it does.

Spiritual and mystical correlations between Bigfoot and humans are prolific. In times of danger the great creature will appear and bring a warning of imminent danger or if one sees a Bigfoot they have been blessed and will make great strides in life. It goes on and on. Some Native American lore says that Bigfoot is a messenger from the great creator, that it has psychic abilities. Some even say Bigfoot is invisible and can transform into many different forms. Some say Bigfoot is good, some say it is bad, some even say it is a cannibalistic man eater who should be feared and worshipped at the same time. But one thing remains constant and that is Bigfoot. Day after day, month after month, year after year the stories keep rolling in. Told by sincere and credible people who are not looking to make financial gain from their information, but who just want to know what it was they saw. What was this huge, upright, bipedal, hairy, manlike, creature that they plainly saw? To actually have a solid numeric statistic as to how many sightings have occurred in history is very hard to state. Using available numbers and then determining a percentage is what is done commonly and with reason. If we step back and look at the numerous online maps that show Bigfoot sightings and we read historical references that tell of what could be interpreted as encounters with the creature, the numbers are huge. As with any strange encounter, it can be safe to assume just as many sightings are never reported or even mentioned. But through it all Bigfoot moves on, walking through our dreams and our consciousness. What if it's all true and every single thought and assumption is valid and factual, and this creature has all the abilities that everyone thinks it does? One thing is certain, we do not know. It is a matter of belief and faith and knowing what we saw with our own eyes. This is where we enter the quagmire of faith and belief. Believing something exists and having faith that it exists are very similar yet serves different purposes to humans. We have needs that we must nurture and in many cases we must use our faith to ease our troubled minds and convince ourselves that what we need will happen, it will come to fruition, and we make ourselves believe that it will. What is the collective power of humanity when it comes to our faith and beliefs? Do we as a species have the ability to collectively make physical changes to ourselves as well as our environment just by all thinking the same thoughts at the same time? Is the collective consciousness real? If enough people think the same thought at the same exact time will this create a reality that can be witnessed? What if the creature known as Bigfoot is a teacher? What if the job of Bigfoot is to teach us how to think, to show us that even though we have been taught to think, we are each isolated creatures existing in our own little bubbles and going through life asleep? If we just wake up and look around, we have amazing abilities, and we can do amazing things with our minds. Maybe Bigfoot sees us as the poor unknowing souls we are; consumed with ego and stumbling through life numbed by greed and destined to destroy ourselves.

This passive creature of the woods, is a creature that exists with, and is a part of, nature. Bigfoot does not fight against anything, just simply lives, walks, eats and sleeps like all creatures do. But because no physical evidence exists, this immediately makes Bigfoot nonexistent due to the fact that we humans cannot find any remains or capture one alive. What a perfect example of an ego based life form that cannot see beyond its nose. Every year numerous new life forms are discovered. Just because Bigfoot is not some small life form that has existed for millions of years and almighty man has just found it does not mean it never existed, it just means we haven't been smart enough or advanced enough to gather the evidence we need to say that it does. Many individuals sit behind desks and become experts on nature and all that happens in the outdoors. They have no need to spend much of their lives in the wilderness as they have all the written information at their disposal and can make conclusions with the information others have gathered. They "think" they understand nature and its diverse and abundant life forms and ecosystems, yet they have never sat in the deep woods in the dead of winter and leaned against an enormous tree and listened when the snow falls. They do not understand the whispers. They do not know how the land talks to you, how the woods tell you what is happening.

A connection exists between the human spirit and all of nature. It is like a rapture that wraps you in it and holds you as you realize you are not alone. You are part of something much bigger than yourself. It is all fairly simple, it doesn't require extensive technical training, it doesn't require years of having your head stuck in books, nor does it require quantum perspectives. How bizarre it would be if one day we had the proof we require to finally understand what Bigfoot is telling us. Is it even possible to teach a fickle, self-destructive creature such as man that we are screwing everything up? Do we have the ability to look at ourselves and realize we are a plague to ourselves and Mother Earth? Can we learn from example and realize something much bigger and much more powerful than us is not out looking to kill or destroy anything, it is only looking to exist and be part of all that is life? Learning to coexist with all creatures takes a deeper understanding of life and all it has to offer. Being a creature that responds or reacts to the unknown by trying to kill what it doesn't understand shows only a regression in intelligence and ignorance with respect to life. Understanding the facts of existence and that everything has a purpose and sometimes that purpose is being food for another creature is just how life is. This is the natural progression of existence, an acceptable procedure that is a Ying within the Yang. Although there are references to Bigfoot being a bad creature that steals souls or is a cannibal, a large number of stories cast the creature in a good light, referring to Bigfoot as a creature that seeks to help not hurt. A creature that comes to us when we need it to be there and in seeing Bigfoot we try to figure out what the meaning of the sighting is in regard to our place in time at that moment. Very few reports show an aggressive creature that is looking to hurt. What the cumulative results from the bulk of the reports show is a creature that seems more curious and non-aggressive than most. So many reports state that the creature was surprised by humans and instead of attacking it fled into the safety of the woods.

One thing that is mentioned over and over by everyone we spoke with is a "feeling." Each person had a feeling about something at the place they were. Whether it was a feeling of forewarning, a feeling of being watched, a feeling of being out of time and place, they all spoke of it. Some mentioned they felt like something bad had happened in the area they were in, some said they felt like something was watching them, actually many said they felt intensely that something was watching them and it made them extremely nervous which was not a good feeling. What is this "feeling" that everyone is having? It is obvious it means something different and specific to each individual even when it is the same feeling. We asked several of the individuals we spoke with how their sighting of Bigfoot affected them and had the encounter changed them in some way. The answer was yes in every case. And in some a profound change took place. The other strange events also resulted in individuals rethinking some aspects of life they had firm beliefs in. As to whether these feelings are part of an intuitive experience or not would be hard to determine. However the feelings these individuals spoke of are strong and caused them to think, react and respond to them in several ways.

Our trip to Kentucky was a great experience. We accomplished our mission which was to gather as much information as possible, interact with as many eyewitnesses and historians as we could in five days. The Reality Entertainment Investigative Team consisted of Philip Gardiner, O.H. Krill, Matt Clark, Tony Gerard, myself and Kat Drake. The team members who had never been to Kentucky were stunned by the beauty of the land and amazed at the generosity and hospitality of the people of Anderson County. To me this was nothing new as I have experienced it all my life. We were also stunned by the night we spent on The X Farmer's land. Events of that night will stay with us forever even though we might never know exactly what happened to us in that field in the middle of the night. We all felt as if something was moving through the trees, but it was not moving in any normal manner, instead it was flowing through the trees in the darkness of night. The Native American Lakotas say the "Bigman" glides through the trees, as if the trees were not there. The X Farmer's nephew stated that what he heard was moving through the trees as if the trees were not there, like it was flying through the trees but in a way he could not understand. Other Native Americans say the Bigfoot/Bigman is of another dimension, and will be with us when we need him. The idea of dimensional travel and Bigfoot is something I think needs to be thought about a great deal.

I have always been a proponent of multiple dimensions. The work of Michio Kaku was like a validation of my thoughts on the possibility of other inter-dimensional realms. At times I have wondered if I was using this theoretical reality as a convenient way to explain the unexplainable. But I think not, I think the probability of multiple existences is as valid as any other. In the world of radio electronics and radio communications, resonance and frequency are a combination that must exist for transmissions to take place. Resonance is the tendency of a system to oscillate at maximum amplitude at a specific frequency. Resonance is about vibrations; everything vibrates and therefore all things have an inherent resonant frequency. Further more, all things on Earth, for example, resonate collectively, meaning that the Earth itself has a unique collective frequency which may indeed be a beacon to other intelligent beings light years away. It's perfectly plausible for another reality to exist right beside us? It would be just as real as the world we live in yet we are completely unaware of it. We could not see or hear it because it existed outside of our ability to acknowledge it and perhaps outside the realm of our senses. As can be expected with something that vibrated and is affected by external forces that can impact its rate or speed of vibration, sometimes the frequency changes and next thing you know we are somewhere we are not supposed to be or something joins us in our existence and we see it. Far out and wacky? Not really, we are very close via nano-technology to making very small things displace themselves in some form, possibly molecular, and then reappear in another place, more or less like the transporter on Star Trek. How insane would this process have been considered just 100 years ago? Most likely someone would have been hanged for blasphemy or burned at a stake for even daring to think of such a thing. Yet now we are close to making this a reality, even if in a micro or nano way. We are close to at least understanding the mechanisms that would make this type of event a reality, we just need to determine how to create the power necessary. But why couldn't a more advanced species have already done it? Or perhaps in another existence in another dimension, this type of inter-dimensional travel is just as common as when we get into our vehicles and drive to the store. We should never limit ourselves with closed minds and never accept impossible as an answer. Is Bigfoot simply a dimensional traveler who enjoys our world as it is well suited for its needs? Someday we will find the answer to all these questions and then we can all sit back and point fingers at each other and some will be able to say "I told you so." And once again ego will override acceptance of the curious mind.

The Frazier Land is a vast area with breathtaking beauty. From the rolling hillsides to the dark and mysterious caves, this area has long been a home to unexplained phenomena. Panther Rock is a cave that seems out of place, I guess saying a cave should be in a certain place or environment is somewhat nonsense but for some reason Panther Rock always gave me that feeling. Then again maybe it is not the cave I am getting that feeling from. Could it be the shadow creature seen by many, could I be feeling something that is lost, on duty or simply waiting? When I saw the bluish, white light come from the cave that night, I was seeing something that wasn't made by man. That light was from somewhere else. It was the color of the light that said it was something unusual, something different. The light had a look to it that was and is hard to describe. Although transparent like a ray of light would be, there was something else about it. It covered a large area and lit from below the tree line on up into it. It shone into the air but came to a halt. It was like it did not dissipate, it just stopped. And when it went out, it was instantly gone, no sounds, no noise, no smell, nothing, just on and then off. Was this the arrival of the shadow creature? Was this the opening of a portal and the entrance of the shadow creature to this old cave and land? Some have asked me why this had such a deep impact on me. They understood it was a very strange event and that it would be very intense to witness this light coming from down below and from the front of this cave, but it seemed to have a very profound impact on me. What I have only told a very few people is that this was not the first time I had seen this light. I had seen this exact odd color in a light once before.

I am now going to tell of the event where I saw the exact same strangely colored bluish, white light. This is taken from when I wrote down what had happened to me many years ago on a cold January night.

I had been up late talking to a friend of mine on 2 meter radio. At about 2 a.m. we signed off and my dog needed to go out. It was mid-January in Kentucky and it was a cold, clear night. I put on a hooded jacket, leashed my dog and headed out my front door. Let me explain the location of the house as it is relevant to this story. My house was on a corner and the front of it pointed exactly east, to the left was north, right was south and of course behind the house was west. In my front yard were two large trees approximately 35-40 feet tall and about 20 feet apart. I opened the door and stepped out behind my dog. The front porch was a small covered porch that had two steps down to the sidewalk. My dog stepped down and I stopped before following him because I was looking up at the sky which was very clear. I suddenly noticed the most bizarre thing - there were shadows moving and an odd bluish light. The shadows moving were from the trees, it was so weird, my dog's head snapped to the left and up, as did mine. What I saw is hard to explain, but I think the best description is that the sky was ripping open. I have spent an endless number of hours watching the sky with all kinds of viewing devices, from large telescopes to binoculars to the naked eye, so I am very familiar with all kinds of activity. But this was something I had never seen. To the north and at about 45 degrees off the horizon was a place in the sky that was square, yet elongated, that was slowly going from left to right. The bluish colored area was filling in the area on the inside. It was the strangest thing I have ever seen. It was moving along at a steady pace inside this square area, and the light from it was making the shadows of the trees move on the ground.

After moving a ways out, it was gone like someone threw a switch. I just stood there in shock. My dog was looking back at me so we stood for a moment while I decided to just walk him and then go back inside the house. We went between the two trees and walked down the street. After he was done, we turned and headed back. He kept looking to the north as we came back and even stopped once, as we approached the street in front of the house. He stopped and just stood there, then he looked back at me and we started walking again. I decided to walk down the driveway instead of walking between the trees, as we approached the point where we would turn right and head to the porch. He stopped again, only this time he growled, a deep rumbling sound, and looked straight up above us. I looked up and couldn't see anything. Then I heard it, and the sound was rather haunting. It was like a distant steam valve releasing slowly above us, but I could see nothing. Suddenly my dog almost yanked me off my feet, even though I am a big guy and my dog weighs around 85 lbs., he practically drug me up the steps and started clawing at the door. We have been together a long time and I have never seen him act like this. I yanked the door open, went in and headed back to my bedroom. For hours he went up and down the hall from my bedroom to the living room, looking out the windows with his ears up like he was on full alert.

Since that night my dog has started looking up into the sky, just like he did then. He will look into the empty night sky and then he will bark and growl and actually stand on his back legs, while he does this. He has done this in several states, but he never does it during the daytime, it is like he knows something is up there, and whatever it is, he doesn't like it. I have no idea what this is, but I think it is some kind of portal or something coming through a rip in time or space. All I know for sure is that something was up in the sky above us, and whatever it was, I absolutely believe came through the rip in the sky. The rip in the sky that I saw that night was exactly the same color as the light that came from the front of the cave at Panther Rock. The house I lived in was no more than one or two miles from The Frazier Land. Whatever the connection between these two events I may never know. However I know that the light emitted from the rip in the sky and the light emitted from the cave at Panther Rock were both unique and I have never seen a light that held the exact look of these two lights.

The summer of 2008 slowly moves on at The X Farmer's land and across all of The Frazier Land. The beauty of Anderson County Kentucky basks in the warm sunshine. So how are things in The Frazier Land since the Reality Entertainment Investigative team went to research the area? In late June The X Farmer decided to put up an electric fence to keep the animals out of his garden. He put the fence up and placed it where he thought it would be touched by the deer and they would then know not to come back and they would leave his garden alone. A day later as The X Farmer and his family sat eating dinner they were startled to hear what sounded like a human screaming. As they were inside the house the loudness of the scream caught them unprepared (as if any scream is something anyone is prepared for). They assumed that it must be a deer that had wandered to the fence and found it was now in place. However they then realized that this scream was not at all like any sound they had ever heard a deer make. This sound was like a person screaming. Two of The X Farmer's sons grabbed their pistols and walked out the front door of the house and headed in the direction of the barn and the area of the fence. As they neared the barn the scream erupted again, and of course this time it was much louder as they were getting closer to it. Although the scream had humanlike qualities, there was still something nonhuman to the sound. The boys each pulled their weapons and stood silent looking in the direction of where the sound was coming from.

They stood quietly and listened for any sounds they could hear, but they heard nothing. From where they stood they could have heard anything moving away through the brush and woods. But they heard nothing. Upon inspecting the area where the fence was they could see nothing to give them a clue what it was that made this sound. The X Farmer said that this area is less than fifty yards from the spot where he took the photo of the eighteen plus inch foot track.

A few weeks ago The X Farmer and his son were standing in his yard late one night talking. The house is surrounded by a fence with a large steel gate that weighs seventy pounds. Suddenly something slammed into the gate with such impact that it shook the fence. The dogs jumped to their feet and one dog actually ran to the house while the other went directly to the gate and started growling. What makes this event even stranger is the fact that the outside of the gated area is lighted and so is the surrounding area. The X Farmer and his son stood staring at nothing, there was nothing near the gate, and nothing could be seen. For something to impact this gate with enough force to do what it did, this would take a large amount of force with weigh behind it. Yet nothing was there. If something was there it would have been easily seen. Could Bigfoot be letting The X Farmer and his family know that it is still around even though it can remain invisible to them, it is still there?

July 18, 2008 The X Farmer called and said something had just happened. He heard an owl in the woods, it was late and the owl sounded odd. The next thing he knew he heard bird's wings flapping over his head. He said the bird's wings must have been huge as the sound was loud, louder than any he had ever heard. He said that whatever the bird was it landed directly above him in a tree, and then made sounds unlike anything he had ever heard. Then there was silence.

There are events regularly occurring in The Frazier Land as they have for hundreds and possibly thousands of years. For now strange is normal to those who live in The Frazier Land, maybe someday strange will be normal for us all …

ABOUT THE AUTHOR

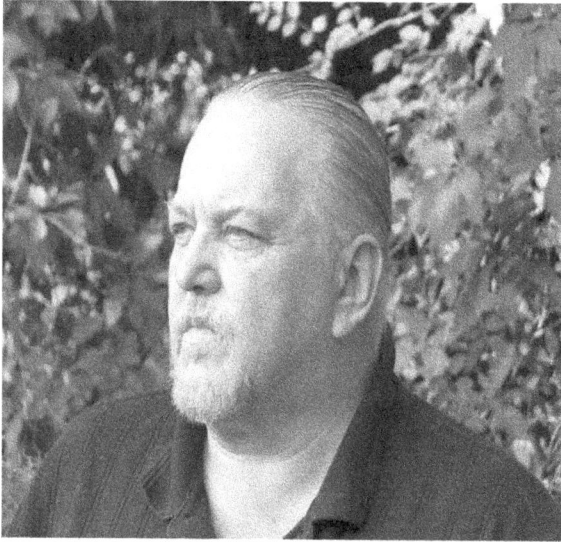

Philip Spencer grew up in Anderson County, Kentucky, in the town of Lawrenceburg. Blessed or cursed with an insatiable curiosity for everything, he has been seeking answers to the mysteries of life, death and the paranormal since childhood.

A 30-year veteran investigator, he has amassed hundreds of case files in his research of strange events that have occurred around the world. He has compiled countless hauntings and spirit activity cases, as well as many remarkable UFO sightings.

Bigfoot however, is the author's preferred area of research as in Anderson County, Kentucky, there have been many sightings of the enigmatic creature known the world over. His first book, *The Wildman of Kentucky, The Mystery of Panther Rock*, entails these sightings and much more, taking the reader on a journey into the heart of the "dark and bloody ground" one of the most active paranormal places in the nation also known as The Frazier Land.

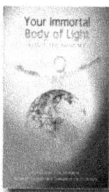

www.ingramcontent.com/pod-product-compliance
Lightning Source LLC
Chambersburg PA
CBHW052040270326
41931CB00012B/2574